Francis Yeats-Brown

Caught by the Turks

Outlook

Francis Yeats-Brown

Caught by the Turks

1. Auflage | ISBN: 978-3-73261-829-3

Erscheinungsort: Paderborn, Deutschland

Erscheinungsjahr: 2018

Outlook Verlag GmbH, Paderborn.

Reproduction of the original.

CAUGHT BY THE TURKS

BY

FRANCIS YEATS-BROWN

WITH PORTRAITS AND PLANS

LONDON

EDWARD ARNOLD

1919

[*All rights reserved*]

To

LADY PAUL

CAUGHT BY THE TURKS

CHAPTER I

CAPTURE

Half an hour before dawn on November the thirteenth, 1915....

We were on an aerodrome by the River Tigris, below Baghdad, about to start out to cut the telegraph lines behind the Turkish position.

My pilot ran his engine to free the cylinders from the cold of night, while I stowed away in the body of the machine some necklaces of gun-cotton, some wire cutters, a rifle, Verey lights, provisions, and the specially prepared map —prepared for the eventuality of its falling into the hands of the Turks—on which nothing was traced except our intended route to the telegraph lines west and north of Baghdad. Some primers, which are the explosive charges designed to detonate the gun-cotton, I carefully stowed away in another part of the machine, and with even more care—trepidation, indeed—I put into my pockets the highly explosive pencils of fulminate of mercury, which detonate the primers which detonate the gun-cotton.

Then I climbed gingerly aboard, feeling rather highly charged with explosives and excitement.

For some time the pilot continued to run his engine and watch the revolution meter. The warmer the engine became, the colder I got, for the prelude to adventure is always a chilly business. Unlike the engine, I did not warm to my work during those waiting moments. At last, however, the pilot waved his hand to give the signal to stand clear, and we slid away on the flight that was to be our last for many a day. The exhaust gases of our engine lit the darkness behind me with a ring of fire. I looked back as we taxied down the aerodrome, and saw the mechanics melting away to their morning tea. Only one figure remained, a young pilot in a black and yellow fur coat, who had left his warm bed to wish us luck. For a moment I saw him standing there, framed in flame, looking after us regretfully. Then I saw him no more, and later they told me (but it was not true) that he had died at Ctesiphon.

We rose over the tents of our camp at Aziziah, all silver and still in the half-light, and headed for the Turkish outposts at El Kutunieh. Their bivouac fires mounted straight to heaven. It was a calm and cloudless dawn, ideal weather for the business we had been sent out to do.

At all costs, we had been told, the telegraphic communications west and north of Baghdad must be cut that day. Von der Goltz and a German battery of quick-firing guns were hasting down from Mosul to help their stricken ally, and reinforcements of the best Anatolian troops, magnificently equipped and organised by the Germans, were on their way from Gallipoli, whence they came flushed with the confidence of success.

Our attack on Ctesiphon was imminent. It was a matter of moments whether the Turkish reinforcements would arrive in time. Delay and confusion in the Turkish rear would have helped us greatly, and the moral and material advantage of cutting communications between Nur-ed-Din, the vacillating Commander-in-Chief defending Baghdad, and Von der Goltz, the veteran of victories, was obvious and unquestionable. But could we do it in an old Maurice Farman biplane?

Desperate needs need desperate measures. The attempt to take Baghdad was desperate—futile perhaps—and contrary to the advice of the great soldier who led the attack in the glorious but unsuccessful action of Ctesiphon. And so also, in a small way, ours was a desperate mission. Our machine could carry neither oil nor petrol enough for the journey, and special arrangements had to be made for carrying spare tins of lubricant and fuel. With these we were to refill at our first halt. While I was destroying the telegraph line, my pilot was to replenish the tanks of his machine. According to the map this should have been feasible, for the telegraph lines at the place we had selected for our demolition ran through a blank desert, two miles from the nearest track. That the map was wrong we did not know.

All seemed quite hopeful therefore. We had got off "according to plan," and the engine was running beautifully.

It was stimulating to see the stir of El Kutunieh as we sailed over the Turks at a thousand feet. They ran to take cover from the bombs which had so often greeted them at sunrise; but for once we sailed placidly on, having other fish to fry, and left them to the pleasures of anticipation. Far behind us a few puffs from their ridiculous apology for an anti-aircraft gun blossomed like sudden flowers and then melted in the sunlight above the world. Below, in the desert, it was still dark. Men were rubbing their eyes in El Kutunieh and cursing us.

But for us day had dawned. As we rose, there rose behind us a round cheerful sun, whose rays caught our trail and spangled it with light, and danced in my eyes as I looked back through the propeller, and lit up the celluloid floor of the nacelle as if to help me see my implements. That dawn was jubilant with hope—I felt inclined to dance. And I sang from sheer exhilaration—a sort of swan song (as I see it now) before captivity. The desert seemed barren no longer. Transmuted by the sunrise those "miles and miles of nothing at all" became a limitless expanse where all the kingdoms of the world were spread out before our eyes. Away to the east the Tigris wound like a snake among the sands; to westward, a huddle of houses and date-palms with an occasional gleam from the gold domes of Kazimain, lay the city of the Arabian Nights, where Haroun al Raschid once reigned, and where now there is hope his spirit may reign again. Baghdad nestled among its date-palms, with little wisps of cloud still shrouding its sleep, all unconscious of the great demonstration it was to give before noon to two forlorn and captive airmen. To the north lay the Great Desert with a hint of violet hills on the far horizon. To the south also lay the Great Desert, with no feature on its yellow face save the scar of some irrigation cut made in the twilight time of history.

But the beauties of Nature were not for us: we were intent on the works of man. There was unwonted traffic across the bridge over the great Arch of Ctesiphon. The enemy river craft were early astir, and so were their antediluvian Archies. These latter troubled us no more than was their wont, but the activity at Qusaibah and Sulman Pak was disquieting. Trains of carts were moving across the river from the right to the left bank. Tugs, gravid with troops, were on their way from Baghdad. In trenches and gun emplacements feverish work was in progress. Like ants at a burrow, men were dragging overhead cover into place. Lines of fatigue parties were marching hither and thither. New support trenches were being dug.

As always, when one saw these things, one longed for more eyes, better eyes, an abler pencil, to record them for our staff. An observer has great responsibilities at times: one cannot help remembering that a missed obstruction, a forgotten emplacement may mean a terrible toll of suffering. Our men would soon attack these trenches, relying largely on our photographs and information…. When, a week later, there rose above the battle the souls of all the brave men dead at Ctesiphon, seeing then with clearer eyes than mine, I pray they forgave our shortcomings and remembered we did our best.

We could not circle over Ctesiphon, in spite of the interest we saw there, until our duty was performed, and had to fly on, leaving it to eastward.

On the return journey, however, we promised ourselves as full an investigation as our petrol supply allowed, and had we returned with our report on what we had seen and done that day, things might have been very different. But what's the use of might-have-beens?

After an hour's flying we sighted the telegraph line that was our objective, but when we approached it more closely a sad surprise awaited us, for instead of the blank surface which the map portrayed, we found that the line ran along a busy thoroughfare leading to Baghdad. Some ten thousand camels, it seemed to my disappointed eyes, were swaying and slouching towards the markets of the capital. We came low to observe the traffic better, and the camels craned their long necks upwards, burbling with surprise at this great new bird they had never seen. The ships of the desert, it seemed to me, disliked the ship of the air as much as we disapproved of them.

Besides the camels, there were ammunition carts and armed soldiers along the road, making a landing impossible. Our demolition would only take three minutes under favourable conditions, but in three minutes even an Arab soldier can be trusted to hit an aeroplane and two airmen at point-blank range.

So we flew westward down the road, looking for a landing ground. Baghdad was behind us now. On our right lay a great lake, and ahead we got an occasional glimpse of the Euphrates in the morning sun. At last—near a mound, which we afterwards heard was Nimrod's tomb—we saw that the telegraph line took a turn to northward, leaving the road by a mile or more. Here we decided to land. Nimrod's tomb was to be the tomb of our activities.

While we were circling down I felt exactly as one feels at the start of a race, watching for the starting gate to rise. It was a tense but delightful moment.

We made a perfect landing, and ran straight and evenly towards the telegraph posts. I had already stripped myself of my coat and all unnecessary gear, and wore sandshoes in case I had to climb a post to get at the insulators. The detonators were in my pocket, the wire clippers hung at my belt. I stooped down to take a necklace of gun-cotton from the floor of the 'bus, and as I did so, I felt a slight bump and a slight splintering of wood.

We had stopped.

I jumped out of the machine, still sure that all was well. Andthen——

Then I saw that our left wing tip had crashed into a telegraph post. Even so the full extent of our disaster dawned slowly on me. I could not believe that we had broken something vital. Yet the pilot was quite sure.

The leading edge of the plane was broken. Our flying days were finished. It had been my pilot's misfortune, far more than his fault, that we had crashed. The unexpected smoothness of the landing ground, and a rear wind that no one could have foreseen, had brought about disaster. Nothing could be done. I stood silent—while hope sank from its zenith, to the nadir of disappointment. Nothing remained—except to do our job.

With light feet but heart of lead, I ran across to another telegraph post, leaving the pilot to ascertain whether by some miracle we might not be able to get our machine to safety. But even as I left him I knew that there was no hope; the only thing that remained was to destroy the line and then take our chance with the Arabs.

By the time I had fixed the explosive necklace round the post, a few stray

Arabs, who had been watching our descent, fired at us from horseback. I set the fuse and lit it, then strolled back to the machine, where the pilot confirmed my worst fears. The machine was unflyable.

Presently there was a loud bang. The charge had done its work and the post was neatly cut in two.

Horsemen were now appearing from the four quarters of the desert. On hearing the explosion the mounted men instantly wheeled about and galloped off in the opposite direction, while those on foot took cover, lying flat on their faces. To encourage the belief in our aggressive force, the pilot stood on the seat of the 'bus and treated them to several bursts of rapid fire.

Meanwhile, I took another necklace of gun-cotton and returned to my demolition. This second charge I affixed to the wires and insulators of the fallen post, so as to render repair more difficult. While I was thus engaged, I noticed that spurts of sand were kicking up all about me. The fire had increased in accuracy and intensity. So accurate indeed had it become that I guessed that the Arabs (who cannot hit a haystack) had been reinforced by regulars. I lit the fuse and covered the hundred yards back to the machine in my very best time (which is about fifteen seconds) to get cover and companionship. A hot fire was being directed on to the machine now, at ranges varying from fifty to five hundred yards. It was not a pleasant situation, and I experienced a curious mixed feeling of regret and relief: regret that there was nothing more to do, relief that something at least had been accomplished to earn the long repose before us. On the nature of this repose I had never speculated, and even now the fate that awaited us seemed immaterial so long as something happened quickly. One wanted to get it over. I was very frightened, I suppose.

Bang!

The second charge had exploded, and the telegraph wires whipped back and festooned themselves round our machine. The insulators were dust, no doubt, and the damage would probably take some days to repair. So far so good. Our job was done in so far as it lay in our power to do it.

"Do you see that fellow in blue?" said the pilot to me, pointing to a ferocious individual about a hundred yards away who was brandishing a curved cutlass. "I think it must be an officer. We had better give ourselves up to him when the time comes."

I cordially agreed, but rather doubted that the time would ever come. It speaks volumes for Arab marksmanship that they missed our machine about as often as they hit it.

I destroyed a few private papers, and then, as it was obviously useless to return the fire of two hundred men with a single rifle, we started up the engine again, more with the idea of doing something than with any hope of getting away.

The machine, it may be mentioned, was not to be destroyed in the event of a breakdown such as this, because our army hoped to be in Baghdad within a week, and it would have been impossible for the Turks to carry it with them in the case of a retreat.

The Arabs hesitated to advance, and still continued to pour in a hot fire. Feeling the situation was becoming ridiculous, I got into the aeroplane and determined to attempt flying it. Now I am not a pilot, and know little of machines. The pilot had pronounced the aeroplane to be unflyable, and very rightly did not accompany me.

But I was pigheaded and determined "to have one more flip in the old 'bus." After disentangling the wires that had whipped round the king posts, I got into the pilot's seat and taxied away down wind. Then I turned, managing the operation with fair success, and skimmed back towards the pilot with greatly increasing speed. But all my efforts did not succeed in making the machine lift clear of the ground. Some Arabs were now rushing towards the pilot, and a troop of mounted gendarmes were galloping in my direction. I tried to swerve to avoid these men, but could not make the machine answer to her controls. Then I pulled the stick back frantically in a last effort to rise above them. She gave a little hop, then floundered down in the middle of the cavalry.

Somehow or other the 'bus was standing still, and I was on the ground beside it.

Mounted gendarmes surrounded me with rifles levelled, not at me, but at the machine. I cocked my revolver and put it behind my back, hesitating. Then an old gendarme spurred his horse up to me and held out his right hand in the friendliest possible fashion. I grasped it in surprise, for the grip he gave me was a grip I knew, proving that even here in the desert men are sometimes brothers. Then, emptying out the cartridges from my revolver in case of accidents, I handed it to him. Not very heroic certainly—but then surrendering is a sorry business: the best that can be said for it is that it is sometimes common sense.

At that moment the gentleman in blue, whose appearance we had previously discussed, suddenly appeared behind me and swinging up his scimitar with both hands, struck me a violent blow where neck joins shoulder. This blow deprived me of all feeling for a moment. On coming-to I discovered that my aggressor was not dressed in blue at all; he wore no stitch of raiment of any description, but whether he was painted with woad or only tanned by the sun I had no opportunity of enquiring. Whether, again, the kindly gendarme had turned the blow or whether the *ghazi* had purposely hit me with the flat of his weapon, I never discovered; but of this much I am certain, that except for that kindly gendarme—to whom may Allah bring blessings—this story would not have been written.

I made my way to the pilot as soon as I was able to do so, and found him bleeding profusely from a wound in the head, surrounded by a hundred tearing, screaming Arabs. Every minute, the number of the Arabs was increasing, and the gendarmes had the greatest difficulty in protecting us. All round us excited horsemen circled, firing *feux de joie* and uttering hoarse cries of exultation. We were making slow progress towards the police post about a mile distant, but at times, so fiercely did the throng press round us, I doubted if we should ever come through.

Once, yielding to popular clamour, the police stopped and parleyed with some Arab chiefs who had arrived upon the scene. After a heated colloquy of which we did not understand one word, in spite of our not unnatural interest, the Turkish gendarmes shrugged their shoulders and appeared to accede to the Arabs' demands. Several of the more ruffianly among them seized the pilot and pulled his flying coat over his head. The memory of that moment is the most unpleasant in my life, and I cannot, try as I will, entirely dissociate myself from the horror of what I thought would happen. Even now it often holds sleep at arm's length. Not the fact of death, but the imagined manner of it, dismayed me. I bitterly regretted having surrendered my revolver only to be thus tamely murdered.

Meanwhile I had been also seized and borne down under a crowd of Arabs. We fought for some time, and I had a glimpse of the pilot, who is a very clever boxer, upholding British traditions with his fists... .

Suddenly the scene changed from tragedy to farce. We were not going to be murdered at all, but only robbed. And the pilot had given our *ghazi* friend a black eye—blacker than his skin.

At length I got free, minus all my possessions except my wrist watch, which they did not see, and saw that the pilot also had his head above the scrimmage, still "bloody but unbowed." The worst was over. That had been the climax of my capture.

All that happened thereafter, until chances of escape occurred, was in a *diminuendo* of emotion.

All I really longed for now was for something to smoke. My cigarette case had gone.

The gendarmes, who had stood aside through these proceedings, now returned and hurried us towards the police post, while most of the captors remained behind disputing about our loot. All this time the machine had been absolutely neglected, but now I saw some Arabs stalking cautiously up to it and discharging their firearms. Feeling the machine would be damaged beyond repair if they continued firing at it, and so rendered useless to us after our imminent capture of Baghdad, I tried to explain to the gendarmes that it was quite unnecessary to waste good lead on it, its potentiality for evil having vanished with our surrender. The impression I conveyed, however, was that there was a third officer in the machine, and a large party adjourned to investigate. During this diversion I tried to jump on to a white mare, whose owner had left her to go towards the machine, but received a second nasty blow on the spine for my pains. Again the kindly gendarme came to my rescue, seeing, I suppose, that I was looking pretty blue. He addressed me as "Baba," and—may Allah give him increase!—gave me a cigarette.

At last we got to the police post, and, as we entered and passed through a dark stable passage, the gendarme on my left side, noticing my wrist watch, slyly detached it and pocketed it with a meaning smile. As the price of police protection I did not grudge it.

Big doors clanged behind us and our captivity proper had begun: what had gone before had been more like a scrum at Rugger, with ourselves as the ball.

We examined our injuries and bruises, and I tried to dress the wounds on the pilot's head, with little success, however, for our guardians could provide nothing but the most brackish water, and disinfectants were undreamed of. We discussed our future at some length, and agreed that our best plan was to be recaptured in Baghdad on the taking of that city. To this end we decided that it would be advisable to make the most of our injuries, so that when the Turkish retreat took place we would not be in a fit condition to accompany it. To feign sickness would not, indeed, be difficult. I felt that every bone in my body was broken, and my pilot was in an even worse condition.

Meanwhile there was a great clamour and "confused noises without," which seemed to refer insistently and unpleasantly to us. On asking what the people were saying, we were informed that the Arabs wanted to take our heads to the Turkish Commander-in-Chief at Suleiman Pak, whereas the gendarmes pointed out that there would be far greater profit and pleasure in taking us there alive. We cordially agreed, and did not join the discussion, feeling it to be more academic than practical, as we were quite safe in the police post.

We had neither hats nor overcoats, but we each still retained our jackets and breeches, though in a very torn condition. I was still in possession of my sandshoes, probably because the Arabs did not think them worth the taking.

Considering things calmly, we felt that we were lucky. This bondage would not last. We would surely fly again, perhaps soon. But for a week or so we must accustom ourselves to new conditions. Everything was strange about us, and it struck me at once how close a parallel there is between the drama of Captivity and the drama of Life. In each case there is a "curtain," and in each case a man enters into a new world whose language and customs he does not know. Almost naked we came to our bondage, dumb, bloody, disconcerted by the whole business. So, perhaps, do infants feel at the world awaiting their ken: it is taken for granted that they enjoy life, and so also our captors were convinced that we should feel delighted at our situation.

"We saved you from the Arabs," we understood them to say, "and now you are safe until the war is over. You need do no more work."

Such at any rate was my estimate of what they said, but being in an unknown tongue, it was only necessary to nod in answer.

Tea was brought to us, sweet, weak tea in little glasses, and we made appreciative noises. Then the kindly gendarme—may he be rewarded in both worlds—brought each of us some cigarettes, in return for which we gave him our brightest smiles, having nothing else to give.

But one could not smile for long in that little room, thinking of the sun and air outside and the old 'bus lying wrecked in the desert. We would have been flying back now; we would have reconnoitred the Turkish lines; we would have been back by nine o'clock to breakfast, bath, and glory....

"It's the thirteenth of the month," groaned the pilot, whose thoughts were similar to mine.

For a long time I sulked in silence, while the pilot, with better manners or more vitality than I, engaged the gendarmes in light conversation, conducted chiefly by gesture. About an hour later (a "day" of the Creation, it seemed to me—and it was indeed a formative time, when the mind, so long accustomed to range free, seeks to adjust its processes to captivity and adapt itself to new conditions of time and space) there occurred at last a diversion to interrupt my gloom.

The Turkish District Governor arrived with two carriages to take us to Baghdad. He spoke English and was agreeable in a mild sort of way, except for his unfortunate habit of asking questions which we could not answer. He told us that news of our descent and capture had been sent to Baghdad by gallopers (not by telegram, I noted parenthetically) and that the population was awaiting our arrival. I said that I hoped the population would not be disappointed, and he assured us with a significant smile that they certainly would not.

"Whatever happens," he was kind enough to add, "I will be responsible for your lives myself."

His meaning became apparent a little later, when we approached the suburbs of Baghdad and found an ugly crowd awaiting our arrival, armed with sticks and stones. When we reached the city itself the streets were lined as if for a royal procession. Shops had put up their shutters, the markets were closed, the streets were thronged, and every window held its quota of heads. The word had gone out that there was to be a demonstration, and the hysteria which lurks in every city in a time of crisis found its fullest scope. Our downfall was taken as an omen of British defeat, and the inhabitants of Baghdad held high holiday at the sight of captive British airmen.

Elderly merchants wagged their white beards and cursed us as we passed; children danced with rage, and threw mud; lines of Turkish women pulled back their veils in scorn, and putting out their tongues at us cried "La, la, la," in a curious note of derision; boys brandished knives; babies shook their little fists. No hated Tarquins could have had a more hostile demonstration. We were both spat upon. A man with a heavy cudgel aimed a blow at my pilot which narrowly missed him, another with a long dagger stabbed through the back of the carriage and was dragged away with difficulty: I can still see his snarling face and *hashish*-haunted eyes. Our escort could hardly force a way for our carriage through the narrow streets. All this time we sat trying to look dignified and smoking constant cigarettes... . State arrival of British prisoners in Baghdad—what a scene it would have been for the cinematograph!

Arrived at the river, a space was cleared round us, and we were embarked with a great deal of fuss in a boat to take us across to the Governor's palace. Before leaving, I said goodbye to the kindly gendarme who had helped a brother in distress, and once more now, across the wasted years of captivity and the turmoil of my life to-day, I grasp his hand in gratitude.

Our first interview in Baghdad was with a journalist. He was very polite and anxious for our impressions, but I told him that the Arabs had given us quite enough impressions for the day, and that words could not adequately express what we felt at our arrival in Baghdad. We chiefly wanted a wash.

That afternoon we were taken to hospital, and to our surprise (for, being new to the conditions of captivity, we were still susceptible to surprise) we found that we were very well treated there. Two sentries, however, stood at our open door day and night to watch our every movement. When the Governor of

Baghdad came to see us that evening (thoughtfully bringing with him a bottle of whisky) I politely told him (in French, a language he spoke fluently) that so much consideration had been shown to us that I hoped he would not mind my asking whether we could not have a little more privacy. The continual presence of the sentries was a little irksome. He understood my point perfectly—much too perfectly. Taking me to the window, he spoke smoothly, as follows:

"I am so sorry the sentries disturb you, but I feel responsible for your safety, and should you by any chance fall out of that window—it is not so very far from the ground, you see—you might get into bad hands. I assure you that Baghdad is full of wicked men."

The Governor was too clever. There was no chance with him of securing more favourable conditions for escape, so we turned to the discussion of the whisky bottle. As in all else he did, he had an object, I soon discovered, in bringing this forbidden fluid. His purpose, of course, was to make us talk, and talk we did, under its generous and unaccustomed influence, for it had been some time since we had seen spirits in our own mess at Azizieh. I would much like to see the report that the Turkish Intelligence Staff made of that wonderful conversation. Several officers had dropped in—casually—to join in the talk, and we told them we had lost our way; then our engine had stopped, and we landed as near to some village as we could. We knew nothing of an attack on Baghdad, we did not know General Townshend, but had certainly heard of him. We had heard a rumour that he had defeated the Turks at Es-sinn a month previously, and would like to know the truth of the matter. Eventually the bottle was exhausted, and so were our imaginations. We parted with the utmost cordiality and a firm intention of seeing as little of each other as possible in the future.

In the street below our window were some large earthenware jars, like those in which the Forty Thieves had hidden aforetime in this very city, and for about a day we considered the story of Aladdin, in regard to the possibility of escape by getting into these jars; but just as we had made our plans the jars were removed, being taken no doubt to the support trenches, which were found by our troops excellently provided with water.

As the day grew near for our attack, we saw many thousand Arabs being marched down to Ctesiphon. It was no conquering army this, no freemen going to defend their native land, but miserable bands of slaves being sent into subjection. Down to the river bank, where they were embarked on lighters, they were followed by their weeping relatives. There was no pretence at heroism. They would have escaped if they could, but the Turks had taken care of that. They were tied together by fours, their right hand being lashed to a wooden yoke, while their left was employed in carrying a rifle. These unfortunate creatures were taken to a spot near the trenches and were then transferred, still securely tied together, to the worst dug and most-exposed part of the line. Machine guns were then posted behind them to block all possible lines of retreat. In addition to minor discomforts such as bearing the brunt of our attack, the Arabs, so I was told, were frequently unprovided with provisions and water, so it is small wonder that their demeanour did not show the fire of battle. But *Kannonen-futter* was required for Ctesiphon, and down the river this pageant of dejected pacifists had to go.

After the attack had begun, shiploads of these same men returned wounded, and arrived in our hospital in an indescribably pitiable condition. There were no stretchers, and the wounded were left to shift for themselves, relying on charity and the providence of Allah. The blind led the blind, the halt helped the lame.

Later, wounded Anatolian soldiers began also to arrive, and their plight was no less wretched than that of the Arabs, though their behaviour was incomparably better. One could not help admiring their stoicism in the face of terrible and often unnecessary suffering. The utter lack of system in dealing with casualties was hardly more remarkable than the fortitude of the casualties themselves. When a proclamation was read to the sufferers in our hospital, announcing the success of the Turkish arms at Ctesiphon, the wounded seemed to forget their pain and the dying acquired a new lease of life. I actually saw a man with a mortal wound in the head, who a few minutes previously had been choking and literally at his last gasp, rally all his forces to utter thanks to God, and then die.

Never for a moment had we thought that the attack on Ctesiphon could fail. The odds, we knew, were heavily against us, but we firmly believed that General Townshend would achieve the impossible. That he did not do so was not his fault nor the fault of the gallant men he led. But this is a record of my personal experiences only, and I will spare the reader all the long reflections and alternations of anxiety and hope which held our thoughts while the guns boomed down the Tigris and the fate of Baghdad—and our fate—was poised in the balance.

At six o'clock one morning we were suddenly awakened and told that we must leave for Mosul immediately. By every possible means in our power we delayed the start, thinking our troops might come at any moment. But the Turkish sergeant who commanded our escort had definite orders that we were to be out of the city by nine o'clock. We drove in a carriage through mean streets, attracting no attention, for now the Baghdadis realised their danger. Before leaving, our sergeant paid a visit to his house, in order to collect his kit, leaving us at the door, guarded by four soldiers. His sisters came down to see him off and (being of progressive tendencies, I suppose) they were not veiled. It were crime indeed to have hidden such lustrous eyes and skin so fair.

CHAPTER II

A SHADOW-LAND OF ARABESQUES

Some breath of reality, some call from the outer world of freedom came to us from the presence of these girls. They seemed the first real people I had seen in my captivity, femininity incarnate, human beings in a shadow-land of arabesques. They were happy and healthy and somehow outside the insanities of our world. For a moment they gazed at us in awe, and for another moment in complete sympathy: then they retired with little squeaks of laughter and busied themselves with their brother's baggage.

When our preparations were complete and we set off on our long journey, they stood for a space at the casement window and waved us goodbye, looking quite charming. I vowed that if Fate by a happy chance were to lead us back to Baghdad with rôles reversed, so that they, not we, were captives in the midst of foes, my first care would be to repay their kindly, though unspoken, sympathy. They were too human for the futilities of war, too amiable to have a hand in Armageddon.

Only prisoners, I think, see the full absurdity of war. Only prisoners, to begin with, fully realise the gift of life. And only prisoners see war without its glamour, and realise completely the suffering behind the lines: the maimed, the blind, the women who weep. Only by a few of us in happy England has the full tragedy of war been realised. Mere words will never record it, but prisoners know "the heartbreak in the heart of things." To us who have been behind the scenes, far from the shouting and the tumult and the captains and the kings, the wretchedness of it all remains indelible. Nothing can make us forget the broken men and women, whose woes will haunt our times.

But I was on the threshold of my experiences then, and the maidens of Baghdad soon passed from memory, I fear—vanishing like the mists of morning that hung over the river-bank at the outset of our journey.

We travelled in that marvellous conveyance, the *araba*. To generalise from types is dangerous, but the *araba* is certainly typical of Turkey. Its discomfort is as amazing as its endurance. It is a rickety cart with a mattress to sit on. A pole (frequently held together by string) to which two ponies are harnessed (frequently again with string) supplies the motive power, which is restrained by reins mended with string, or encouraged by a whip made of string. The contrivance is surmounted by a patchwork hood tied down with string. A few buckets and hay nets are strung between its crazy wheels. Such is the *araba*.

How it holds together is a mystery as inscrutable as the East itself. If all the vitality expended in Turkey on starting upon a journey and continuing upon it were turned to other purposes, the land might flourish. But the philosophy which makes the *araba* possible makes other activities impossible.

A full two hours before the start, when the world is still blue with cold, travellers are summoned to leave their rest. Then the drivers begin to feed their ponies. When this is done they feed themselves. Then, leisurely, they load the baggage. Finally, when all seems ready, it occurs to somebody that it is impossible to leave before the cavalry escort is in saddle. "Ahmed Effendi" is called for. Everyone shouts for "Ahmed Effendi," who is sleeping soundly, like a sensible man. He wakes, and, to create a diversion perhaps, accuses a driver of stealing his chicken. The driver replies in suitable language. Meanwhile time passes. The disc of the sun cuts the horizon line of the desert, disclosing us all standing chill and cramped and bored and still unready. A pony has lain down in his harness, in an access of boredom, no doubt. A goat has stolen part of my scanty bread ration and is now browsing peacefully in the middle distance. Far away a cur is barking at the jackals. Some of our escort have retired to pray, others are still wrangling. Two or three are engaged in kicking the bored pony.

After recovering from the goat my half-loaf, which is so much better than no bread in the desert, I watch with amazement the Turkish treatment of the pony. A skewer is produced and rammed into the unfortunate animal's left nostril. So barbarous does this seem that I am on the point of protesting, when suddenly the animal struggles to its feet, and stands shivering and wide-eyed and apparently well again. After the wound has been sponged and the pony given a few dates, it seems equal to fresh endeavour. The blood-letting has cleared its brain—and no wonder, poor beast.

At length all seems ready. We climb into the *araba*. But we are not off yet. We sit for another hour while the drivers refresh themselves with a second breakfast. A rhyme keeps running through my frozen brain:

> "Slow pass the hours—ah, passing slow—
> My doom is worse than anything
> Conceived by Edgar Allan Poe."

But I did not realise then how lucky we were to be travelling by carriages at all. Nor did I realise what an honour it was to be presented to the local governors through whose districts we passed. It was only late in captivity, when merged in an undistinguished band of prisoners, that I understood the pomp and circumstance of our early days. Late in 1915 a prisoner was still a new sort of animal to the Turks. They were curious about us, and to some extent the curiosity was mutual. One kept comparing them with the descriptions in "Eöthen."

Proceedings generally opened in a long low room. The local magnate sat at a desk, on which were set a saucer containing an inky sponge, a dish of sand, and some reed-pens. A scribe stood beside the *kaimakam* and handed him documents, which he scrutinised as if they were works of art, holding them delicately in his left hand as a connoisseur might consider his porcelain. Then with a reed-pen he would scratch the document, still holding it in the palm of his hand, and after sprinkling it carefully with sand would return it to the scribe. All this was incidental to his conversation with us or with other members of the audience. There were never less than ten people in any of the rooms in which we were interviewed, and as they all made fragmentary remarks, one quoting a text from the Koran, another a French *bon mot*, and a third introducing some question of local politics, and as the governor asked us questions and signed papers and kept up a running commentary with his friends, one felt exactly like Alice at the Hatter's tea party.

"A Turk does not listen to what you are saying," I have since been told, "he merely watches your expression." That this is true of the uneducated I have no doubt, and if correct about the educated Turk I daresay it is not to his discredit. Demeanour in Oriental countries counts for much.

But at Samarra our demeanour was sorely tried. We had been travelling about three days in the desert, when we arrived at this desolate and dishevelled spot. I longed to lie down and shut my eyes, and forget about captivity for a bit, but no!—there came a summons to attend the ghastly social function I had already learned to loathe.

The Governor of that place was a *tout à fait civilisé* Young Turk, sedentary, Semitic, and very disagreeable.

"Is it true that you dropped bombs on the Mosque at Baghdad?" he asked.

And—

"Do you know that the population of Baghdad nearly killed you?"

And—

"Do you know that in another month the English will be driven into the Persian Gulf?" … and so on.

We denied these soft impeachments, and then his method became more direct.

"Some of your friends have been killed and captured," he said—"the commandant of your flying corps, for instance."

Seeing us incredulous, he accurately described the Major's appearance.

"And there is someone else," the *kaimakam* continued in slow tones that iced my blood. "Someone who may be a friend of yours. A young pilot in a fur coat."

My heart stood still.

"He was killed by an Arab," the *kaimakam* added... .

Here I will skip a page or two of mental history. The defeat of my country, the death of my friend, the crumbling of my hopes: little indeed was left... ...

Let five dots supply the ugly blank. There is sorrow and failure enough in the world without speculating on tragedies that never happened. Baghdad was taken later, my friend proved to be captured, not killed, and I write this by Thames-side, not the Tigris.

The inhabitants of Samarra are, I believe, the most ill-balanced people in the world. This trait is well known to travellers, and we found it no traveller's tale. On first arriving at Samarra, we halted in the rest-house on the right bank of the river, and were enjoying our frugal meal of bread and dates when a sergeant came to us from the Governor with orders that we were to be instantly conveyed to his residence, which is situated in the town across the river. We demurred, and our own sergeant protested, but the Governor's emissary had definite orders, and we were hurried down in the twilight. Here we found that there was no boat to take us across. The Samarra sergeant shouted to a boatful of Arabs, floating down the river, but they would not stop. Louder and louder he shouted, till his voice cracked in a scream. Growing frantic with rage, he fired his revolver at the Arabs. Of course he missed them, but the bullets, ricochetting in the water, probably found a billet in the town beyond. The Arab occupants merely laughed in their beards. We also laughed. Then the sergeant declared that we would have to swim, and we urged him in pantomime to show the way.

Eventually he spied a horse-barge down river, with a naked boy playing beside it. Reloading his revolver, a few shots in his direction attracted the lad's attention. Then an old man came out of a hut by some melon beds, to see who was firing at his son.

Another shot or two and the old man and the boy were prevailed upon to take us across. We had secured our transport at last, and the whole transaction seemed (in Samarra) as simple as hailing a taxi.

I bought a melon from the boy, and he snatched my money contemptuously. To take things without violence is a sign of weakness in Samarra. I noticed afterwards that all the boys and girls in this happy spot were fighting each other or engaged in killing something. And their elders keep something of the feckless violence of youth. I do not think that there are any good Samarratans.

After the interview with the Governor already mentioned, which ended by a refusal on our part to speak with him further, we were sent to pass the night in a filthy hovel, whose only furniture consisted of a bench and a chair. Our sergeant was sitting on this chair when an officer rushed in and jerked it from under him, leaving him on the floor. As a conjuring trick it was neat, but as manners, deplorable. We were glad to get away from the place.

Very few incidents came to diversify the monotony of our desert travel. One day, however, we met some Turkish cavalry going down to the siege of Kut. They were a fine body of troops, a little under-mounted perhaps, but thoroughly business-like. Their officers were most chivalrous cavaliers. Here in the desert, where luxuries were not to be had for money or for murder, they frequently gave us a handful of cigarettes, or a parcel of raisins, or else halted their squadron and asked us to share their meal. With these men one felt at ease. They were soldiers like ourselves. They did not ask awkward questions, and were told no lies. I remember especially one afternoon in the Marble Hills when we sat in a ring drinking tea and smoking cigarettes, with the panorama of the desert spread out before us, from the southward plains of Arabia to the hills of the devil-worshippers, misty and mysterious, in the north. We talked about horses all the time. A modern Isaiah delivered himself of the following sentiment, in which I heartily concur:

"Where there is no racing the people perish."

The first-line Turk has many fine qualities, of which generosity and gallantry are not the least. Something in Anglo-Saxon blood is in sympathy with the adventure-loving, flower-loving Turk. But, alas! there is another type of Ottoman, with the taint of Tamerlane. "When he is good he is very very good, but when he is bad he is horrid."

In the latter category I must regretfully place the sergeant who commanded our escort. He came of decent stock (to judge by his charming sisters, and his own appearance indeed) but his mind was all mud and blood. He had been Hunified. Turkey would always be fighting, he said. The English were almost defeated. The Armenians were almost exterminated. But the Greeks remained to be dealt with, and the cursed Arabs. Finally the Germans themselves. In an apotheosis of Prussianism Turkey was to turn on her Allies and drive them out. Such was his creed. But a glow of courage lit the dark places of his mind. He loved fighting for the sheer fun of the thing. A few days beyond Samarra we were attacked by some wandering Arabs, who swept down on us in a crescent. Our guards panicked, but he stood his ground, and, seizing a rifle, dispersed the enemy by some well-directed shots. Whether we were near deliverance or death on that occasion I do not know, but that the panic amongst our escort was not wholly unreasonable was evinced by the fact that only a few hours earlier we had passed the headless trunk of a gendarme, strapped upon a donkey. He had been decapitated as a warning to the Samarratans that two can play at the game of savagery.

The sight of the corpse had unnerved our guard, and as for myself, I did not know whether to be glad or sorry when the Arabs attacked us. To be taken by them meant either going back to the English or to the dust from which we came. The alternative was too heroic to be agreeable. Contrariwise, I was much disappointed when our sergeant finally drove them off. That evening, as if to point the moral, we found the body of another gendarme, also murdered, lying on a dung-heap outside the rest-house. This was at Shergat, the former capital of the Assyrians, and now a squalid village, where, however, the widows of Ashur were still "loud in their wail."

Here we dined with the fattest man I have ever seen. He was really a pig personified, but as we both gobbled out of the same dish and ate the same salt, I will not further enlarge on his appearance.

In the upper reaches of the Tigris there are wild geese so tame that they come waddling up to inspect the rare travellers through their land. I thought it might be possible to catch one of these animals on foot. Coquettishly enough they kept a certain distance. "We don't mind your looking at us," they seemed to say, "but we *do* object to being pawed about." With the coming of the railway I am afraid a gun will destroy their belief in human kind.

The geese appeared to enjoy the smell of sulphuretted hydrogen, which prevails in these regions. The whole country is rich in natural oils and bitumen. One day it will make somebody's fortune, no doubt, and then the geese will waddle away from perspiring prospectors.... .

Before we arrived at Mosul we stopped for a bath at the hot springs of Hammam-Ali, where we met (in the water) a patriarch with a white beard, who confidently assured us that he was a hundred years old and would continue to live for another hundred, such were the beneficent properties of the water. Before his days are numbered he may live to see a Hydro at Hammam-Ali—poor old patriarch. He told us a lot about Jonah (whose tomb is at Nineveh, just opposite Mosul, on the other side of the river), and I am not sure that he did not claim acquaintance with that patriarch. He was quite one of the family.

Mosul, he told us, was a heaven on earth, a land flowing with milk and honey, where we should ride all day on the best horses of Arabia, and feast all night in gardens such as the blessed *houris* might adorn.

It was with a certain elation, therefore, that I saw the distant prospect of

Mosul next morning, set in its surrounding hills. A fair city it seemed, white and cool, with orange groves down to the river and many date-trees. But a closer acquaintance brought cruel disappointment, as generally happens in the East. The blight of the Ottoman was everywhere; there was dirt, decrepitude, and decay in every corner. Children with eye-disease, and adults with leprosies more terrible than Naaman's jostled each other in the mean streets. Whole quarters of the city had given up the ghost, and become refuse heaps, where curs grouted amongst offal. Mosul, like our escort-sergeant's mind, seemed a muddle of mud and blood.

With sinking hearts we drove to the barracks, and were shown into a dark, gloomy office, where our names were taken. Thence we were led to a still murkier and more mouldering room, inhabited—nay, infested—by some ten Arabs. Through this we passed into a cell with windows boarded up, which was, if possible even damper, darker, and more dismal than anything we had yet seen. After the sunlight and great winds of the desert we stood bewildered. Death seemed in the air.

Then out of the gloom there rose two figures. They were British officers, who had been captured about a month previously. So changed and wasted were they that even after we had removed the boards from the little window we could hardly recognise them. One of these officers was so ill with dysentery that he could hardly move, the other had high fever.

Our arrival, with news from the outer world, bad though it was, naturally cheered them considerably, for nothing could be worse than their present plight.

The ensuing days called for a great moral effort on our part. It was absolutely imperative to laugh, otherwise our surroundings would have closed in on us…
. We cut up lids of cigarette boxes for playing cards. We inked out a chessboard on a plank. We held a spiritualistic séance with a soup-bowl, there being no table available to turn. We told interminable stories. We composed monstrous limericks; and we sang in rivalry with the Arab guard outside, who made day hideous with their melody and murdered sleep by snoring.

But when there is little to eat and nothing to do, time drags heavily. Two cells with low ceilings that leaked were allotted to the four of us. In these we lived and ate and slept, except for fortnightly excursions to the baths. We were allowed no communication with the men, who lived in a dungeon below. Their fate was a sealed book to us. We had nothing to read. Under these conditions one begins to fear one's brain, especially at night. It was then that it began to run like a mechanical toy. Like a clockwork mouse, it scampered aimlessly amongst the dust of memory, then suddenly became inert, with the works run down. I grew terrified of thinking, especially of thinking about my friend in the fur coat.

The night hours are the worst in captivity. One lies on the floor, waiting for sleep to come, but instead of blessed sleep, "beloved from pole to pole," thoughts come crowding thick and fast on consciousness, thoughts like clouds that lower over the quiescent body. Each second then seems of inconceivable duration. But there is no escape from Time.

During the day, however, things were more bearable, and occasional gleams of humour enlivened the laggard moments.

Among our guard there were several sentries who (I thought) might conceivably help us to escape. One dark night, one of these men whispered the one word "Jesus," and made the sign of the Cross, as I passed him. After this introduction I naturally hoped that he might be of use. He was a fine figure of a man, with a proud poise of head, and aquiline nose, as if some Assyrian god had been his ancestor. I was gazing at him in admiration the next day, and gauging his possibilities through my single eye-glass, when a curious thing happened.

Our eyes met. He seemed mesmerised by my monocle. For a long time we stared at each other in silence, then, thinking the sergeant of the guard would notice our behaviour, I discreetly dropped my eye-glass and looked the other way. The sentry's mouth quivered as if I had made a joke, but instead of smiling, he burst suddenly into a storm of tears. The sergeant of the guard (a swart, sturdy little Turk) rushed out to see what had happened. There was the big sentry, wailing, and actually gnashing his white teeth. I stood awkwardly, looking as innocent as I felt. The sergeant bristled like a terrier, pulled the sentry's poor nose, and boxed his beautiful ears, while the victim continued to blubber and look piteously in my direction.

But I could not help him at all. I had not the slightest idea what was the matter, nor do I know now. Hysteria, I suppose.

Eventually that great solvent of perplexity, nicotine, came to relieve the awkward situation. First the sergeant accepted a cigarette, then, more diffidently, the sentry. Later I put in my eye-glass again, and convinced them, I think, that its use did not involve the weaving of any unholy spell.

This eye-glass, by the way, survived all the fortunes of captivity. Through it I surveyed the moon-lit plains beyond the Tigris when I planned escape in Mosul, as shall be told in the next chapter. Later it scanned the desert's dusty face for any hope of release. At Afion-kara-hissar it helped me search for a pathway through our guards. At Constantinople it was still my friend. Through it, a month before escape, I looked at the slip of new moon that swung over San Sophia on the last day of Ramazan, wondering where the next moon would find me. And when the next moon came, I watched the sentries by its aid, on the night of our first escape. And it was in my eye when I slipped down the rope to freedom.

But this chapter is getting "gaga." It has a happy ending, however.

One evening when the

> "… little patch of blue,
> That prisoners call the sky"

had turned to sulky mauve, and the air was heavy with storm, and our fellow-prisoners were depressed, and the Arab guard was bellowing songs outside, and we were peeling potatoes for our dinner by the flicker of lamp-light, and life seemed drab beyond description, there came great news to us. Two other officers had arrived.

Next moment they peered into our den, even as we had done. And they were angry, amazed, unshaven, bronzed by the desert air, even as we had been. There in the doorway, ruddy and fair and truculent like some Viking out of time and place, stood the young pilot I had last seen at Aziziah. He was alive, my friend in the fur coat.

The desert had delivered up its dead!

CHAPTER III

THE TERRIBLE TURK

One draws a long breath thinking of those days of Mosul. But bad as our case was, it was as nothing compared with that of the men.

Some two hundred of them lived in a cellar below our quarters, through scenes of misery, and in an atmosphere of death which no one can conceive who does not know the methods of the Turk. Even to me, as I write in England, that Mosul prison begins to seem inconceivable. Huddled together on the damp flag-stones of the cellar, our men died at the rate of four or five a week. Although the majority were suffering from dysentery they not only could not secure medical attention, but were not even allowed out of their cells for any purpose whatever. Their pitiable state can be better imagined than described. Many went mad under our eyes. Deprived of food, light, exercise, and sometimes even drinking water, the condition of our sick and starving men was literally too terrible for words.

It is useless, however, to pile horror on horror. Sixty per cent. of these men are dead, and this fact speaks for itself. No re-statement can strengthen, and no excuse can palliate, the case against the Turks. Our men in this particular instance were killed by the cynical brutality of Abdul Ghani Bey, the commandant of Mosul, and his acquiescent staff.

There is an idea that "the Turks treated their own soldiers no better than our prisoners"; but this is a fallacy—at any rate with regard to hell-hounds such as Abdul Ghani Bey. He took an especial pleasure in inflicting the torments of thirst, hunger, and dirt upon the miserable beings under his care. Animals, in another country, would have been kept cleaner and better fed.

Never shall I forget the arrival in January 1915 of a party of English prisoners from Baghdad. About two hundred and fifty men, who had been captured on barges just before the siege of Kut, had been taken first to Baghdad and thence by forced marches to Kirkuk, a mountain town on the borders of the Turko-Persian frontier. Why they were ever sent to Kirkuk I do not know, unless indeed it was thought that the sight of prisoners suitably starved would re-assure the population regarding the qualities of the redoubtable English soldier. After being exhibited to the population of Kirkuk our men continued their journey, through the bitter cold of the mountains, barefoot and in rags, arriving at last at Mosul shortly after the New Year. Only eighty men then remained out of the original two hundred and fifty, but although their numbers had dwindled their courage had not diminished.

First there marched into our barrack square some sixty of our soldiers in column of route. They were erect and correct as if they were marching to a king's parade. Surely so strange a column will never be seen again. All were sick, and the most were sick to death. Some were barefoot, some had marched two hundred miles in carpet slippers, some were in shirt-sleeves, and all were in rags; one man only wore a great-coat, and he possessed no stitch of clothing beneath it. But through all adversity they held their heads high among the heathen, and carried themselves with the courage of a day "that knows not death." Silently they filed into the already crowded cellar, out of our sight, and many never issued again into the light of the sun.

After these sixty men had disappeared the stragglers began to stagger in. One man, delirious, led a donkey on which the dead body of his friend was tied face downwards. After unstrapping the corpse he fell in a heap beside it. Dysentery cases wandered in and collapsed in groups on the parade ground. An Indian soldier, who had contracted lockjaw, kept making piteous signs to his mouth, and looking up to the verandah, where we stood surrounded by guards. But no one came to relieve those sufferers, dying by inches under our eyes.

That night we managed, by bribing the guards, to have smuggled upstairs to us at tea-time two non-commissioned officers from among the new arrivals. Needless to say, we spent all our money (which was little enough in all conscience) in providing as good a fare as possible, and our famished guests devoured the honey and clotted cream we had to offer. Then one of them suddenly fainted. When he had somewhat recovered he had to be secretly conveyed below, and that was the end of the party—the saddest at which I have ever assisted. The officer who carried the sick man down spent several hours afterwards in removing vermin from his own clothes, for lice leave the moribund, and this poor boy died within a few days.

Sometimes, when our pay was given us, or there occurred an opportunity to bribe our guard, it was our heart-breaking duty to decide which of the men we should attempt to save, by smuggling money to them out of the slender funds at our disposal, and which of their number, from cruel necessity, were too near their end to warrant an attempt to save.

Something of the iron of Cromwell enters one's mind as one writes of these things. If we forget our dead, the East will not forget our shame. Sentiment must not interfere with justice. Abdul Ghani Bey, who shed our prisoners' blood, must pay the penalty. He is the embodiment of a certain type—perhaps not a very common type—of Turk, but common or not, he is one of the men responsible for the terrible death-rate among our soldiers. A short description of him, therefore, will not be out of place.

He was a small man, this tiny Tamerlane, with a limp, and a scowl, and bandy legs. His sombre, wizened face seemed to light with pleasure at scenes of cruelty and despair. He insulted the old, and struck the weak, and delighted in the tears of women and the cries of children. This is not hyperbole. I have seen him stump through a crowd of Armenian widows and their offspring, and after striking some with his whip, he pushed down a woman into the gutter who held a baby at her breast. I have seen him pass down the ranks of Arab deserters, lashing one in the face, kicking another, and knocking down a third. I have seen him wipe his boots on the beard of an old Arab he had felled, and spur him in the face. I hope he has already been hanged, because only the hangman's cord could remove his atavistic cruelty.

His subordinates went in deadly fear of him, and while it was extremely difficult to help our men, it was practically impossible to help ourselves at all in the matter of escape. Yet escape was doubly urgent now, to bring news of our condition to the outer world.

After much thought I decided that a certain wall-eyed interpreter who came occasionally to buy us food was the most promising person to approach. My friend and I laid our plans carefully. After a judicious tip, and some hints as to our great importance in our own country, we evinced a desire to have private lessons with him in Arabic, enlarging at the same time upon the great career that a person like himself might have had, had he been serving the English and not the Turks. Gradually we led round to the subject of escape. At first we talked generalities in whispers, and he was distinctly shy of doing anything of which the dear commandant would not approve; but eventually, softly and distinctly, and with a confidence that I did not feel, I made a momentous proposal to him, nothing less than that he could help us to escape. He winced as if my remark was hardly proper, and fixed me with a single, thunder-struck eye. Then he quavered:

"This is very sudden!"

We could not help laughing.

"This is no jesting matter," he said. "I will be killed if I am caught."

"But you won't get caught. With the best horses in Arabia and a guide like you... ."

"Hush, hush! I must think it over."

For several days he preserved a tantalising silence, alternately raising our hopes by a wink from his wonderful eye, and then dashing them to the ground by a blank stare.

We lived in a torment of hope deferred.

But time passed more easily now. The nights took on a new complexion, flushed by the hope of freedom. From our little window I could see across a courtyard to a patch of river. Beyond it, immense and magical under the starlight, were the ruins of former civilisation—the mounds of Nineveh, the tomb of Jonah, and the rolling downs that lead to the mountains of Kurdistan. To those mountains my fancy went. If sleep did not come, then there were enthralling adventures to be lived in those mountains, adventures of the texture of dreams, yet tinged with a certain prospective of reality... . We had bought revolvers, our horses were ready, we had bribed our guard. We rode far and fast, with our wall-eyed friend as guide. By evening we were in a great forest...

But reality proved a poor attendant on romance. A sordid question of money was our stumbling-block, and a high enterprise was crippled—not for the first or last time—by want of cash. We had already given the interpreter five pounds (which represented so much bread taken out of our mouths), but now he stated that further funds were indispensable to arrange preliminaries. This seemed reasonable, for arms and horses could not be secured on credit in Mosul. Unfortunately, however, funds were not available. We could not, in decency, borrow from other prisoners to help us in our escape. At this juncture our guide, philosopher, and friend lost—or embezzled—a five-pound note that had been entrusted to him by another prisoner to buy us food. Whether he lost it carelessly or criminally I am not prepared to state, but the fact remains he lost it. Our fellow-prisoner very naturally complained to the Turks, as the absence of this five pounds meant we could buy no food for a week.

The Turks arrested the interpreter. He grew frightened, invented a story about the complainant having asked him to help in an escape, then recanted, vacillated, contradicted himself, and got himself bastinadoed for his pains.

The bastinado, I may as well here explain, is administered as follows: the feet of the victim are bared, and his ankles are strapped to a pole. The pole is now raised by two men to the height of their shoulders. A third man takes a thick stick about the diameter of a man's wrist, and strikes him on the soles of the feet. Between twenty and a hundred strokes are administered, while the victim writhes until he faints. No undue exertion is necessary on the part of the executioner, for even after a gentle bastinado a man is not expected to be able to walk for several days.

The wall-eyed interpreter was brought limping to our cell about three days after his punishment. He was brought by Turkish officers, who wished to hear from our own lips a denial of his story that we had been plotting an escape.

It was a dramatic, and for me rather dreadful, moment. Indignantly and vehemently we denied ever having asked his help. Only myself and another, besides the interpreter, knew the truth. To the other officers at Mosul (there were nine of us then, sharing two little cells) this black business is only now for the first time made known. Their indignation, therefore, was by no means counterfeit.

"The man must be mad. No one ever dreamed of escaping," I stated, looking fixedly into the interpreter's one eye, which, while it implored me to tell the truth, seemed to hold a certain awe for a liar greater than himself.

"But——" he stammered, cowed by the circumstance that for once in his life he was telling the truth.

"But what?" we demanded angrily. "Let the villain speak out. His story is monstrous."

"Besides, we are so comfortable here," I added parenthetically.

Eventually the wretched man was led gibbering to an underground dungeon. What happened to him afterwards I do not know. I publish this story after careful thought, because, if he was "playing the game" by us, why did he talk to the Turks about escape? If, on the other hand, he was a prison spy, then his punishment is not my affair.

The treachery of the interpreter was an ill wind for everyone, for our guards were sent away to the front (which is tantamount to a sentence of death) and the vigilance of our new guards was greater than that of the old. Intrigue was dead and our isolation complete.

In these circumstances it may be imagined with what excitement I received the news that the German Consul wanted to see me in the commandant's office. It was the first time for a fortnight that I had left my cell.

I entered slowly, and after saluting the company present, first generally, and then individually, I took a dignified seat after the manner of the country. Ranged round the room were various notables of Mosul—doctors, apothecaries, priests, and lawyers. On a dais slightly above us sat the Consul and the commandant. For some time we kept silence, as if to mark the importance of the occasion. Then a cigarette was offered me by the commandant. I refused this offering, rising in my chair and saluting him again.

At last the German Consul spoke.

He had been instructed by telegraph, he told me, to pay me the sum of five hundred marks in gold. The money came from a friend of my father's. I begged him to thank the generous donor, and a whole vista of possibilities immediately rose to my mind.

The money would be given me next day, the Consul continued, and a *kavass* of the Imperial Government would go with me into the *bazaar* to make any purchases I required.

This conversation took place in French, a language of which the commandant was quite ignorant, and I saw that here was an ideal opportunity for bringing the plight of our prisoners to light. But the Consul, I gathered, wanted to keep on friendly terms with the Turks. Some of the things I told him, however, made him open his eyes, and may have made his kultured flesh creep.

"I will come again to-morrow," he said hurriedly—"you can tell me more then."

After this he spoke in Turkish at some length to the commandant, while the latter interjected that wonderful word *yok* at intervals.

Yok, I must explain, signifies "No" in its every variation, and is probably the most popular word in Turkish. It is crystallised inhibition, the negation of all energy and enthusiasm, the motto of the Ottoman Dilly and Dallys. Its only rival in the vocabulary is *yarin*, which means "to-morrow."

"Yok, yok, yok," said the commandant, and I gathered that he was displeased.

That night I made my plans, and when summoned to the office next day I was armed with three documents. The first was a private letter of thanks to Baron Mumm for his generous and kindly loan. The second was a suggestion that the International Red Cross should immediately send out a commission to look after our prisoners at Mosul. And the third was a detailed list of articles required by our men, with appropriate comments. Items such as this figured on the list:

Soap, for two hundred men, as they had been unable to wash for months.

Kerosene tins, to hold drinking-water, which was denied to our prisoners.

Blankets, as over 50 per cent. had no covering at all.

These screeds startled the company greatly. The Consul stared and the commandant glared, for the one hated fuss and the other hated me. I was delightfully unpopular, but when an Ambassador telegraphs in Turkey, the provinces lend a respectful ear. My voice, crying in the wilderness, must needs be heard.

Summoning an interpreter, the commandant demanded whether I had any cause for complaint; whereupon the following curious three-cornered conversation took place—so far as I could understand the Turkish part:

"The men must be moved to better quarters," said I. "Until this is arranged nothing can be done."

"He says nothing can be done," echoed the interpreter.

"Then of what does he complain?" asked the commandant.

"The very beasts in my country are better cared for," I said. "Our men are dying of hunger and cold."

"He says the men are dying of cold," said the interpreter, shivering at his temerity in mentioning the matter.

"The weather is not my fault," grumbled the commandant, "perhaps it will be better to-morrow. Yes, *yarin*."

And so on. Talk was hopeless, but before leaving I gave the German Consul to understand that he now shared with Abdul Ghani Bey the responsibility for our treatment. To his credit, be it said, the commandant was removed shortly after our departure.

Two days after this interview we were moved from Mosul, where our presence was becoming irksome no doubt. Before leaving I left all my fortunate money, except five pounds, with the Consul, asking him to form a fund (which I hoped would be supplemented later by the Red Cross) for sick prisoners. Twelve months later this money was returned to me in full, but I fancy that it had done its work in the meanwhile.

On the day before our journey I went shopping with the Imperial *kavass* aforesaid, and it was a most pompous and pleasant excursion. Although I wore sandshoes and tattered garments, what with my eyeglass, and the gorgeous German individual, dressed like a Bond Street *commissionaire*, who carried my parcels and did my bargaining, I think we made a great impression upon the good burgesses of Mosul.

We threaded our way among Kurds with seven pistols at their belts, and Arabs hung with bandoliers, and astonishing Circassians with whiskers and swords. Almost every male swaggered about heavily armed, but a blow on their bristling midriff would have staggered any one of them. Their bark, I should think, is worse than their bite.

After a Turkish bath, where I graciously entertained the company with coffee, we strolled round the transport square, where we chaffered hotly for carriages to take us to Aleppo.

The material results of the morning were:

Some food and tobacco for the men staying behind.

Rations for ourselves, consisting of an amorphous mass of dates, cigarettes, conical loaves of sugar, candles, and a heap of unleavened bread.

Carriages for our conveyance to Aleppo.

But the moral effect of our excursion was greater far. I sowed broadcast the seeds of disaffection to Abdul Ghani Bey. To the tobacconist I said that the English, Germans, Turks, and all the nations of the earth, while differing in other matters, had agreed he was a worm to be crushed under the heel of civilisation. To the grocer I repeated the story. To the fruiterer I said his doom was nigh, and to the baker and candlestick maker that his hour had come.

Everyone agreed. *Conspuez le commandant* was the general opinion.

"In good old Abdul Hamid's days," they said, "such devil's spawn would not have been allowed to live."

It was a matter of minutes before rumours of his downfall were rife throughout the city.

Next day he came to see us off, bow-legs, whip, and scowl and all. He stood stockily, watching us drive away, and then turned and spat. But the taste of us was not to be thus easily dispelled. He will remember us, I hope, to his dying day. May that day be soon!

CHAPTER IV

"OUT OF GREAT TRIBULATION…."

We had left a sad party of prisoners behind us, alas! but we had done what little we could for them. Confined as we had been, their sufferings had only added to our own. The best hope for them lay in the German Consul. He could do more, if he wished, than we could have achieved for all our wishes. Nothing could have been more hopeless than our position at Mosul. But now at least there was the open road before us, and hope, and health.

The desert air is magnificent. The untamed winds seemed to blow through every fibre of one's being, and clear away the cobwebs of captivity. The swinging sun, the great spaces of sand, the continuous exercise, and the lean diet of dates and bread, produce a feeling of perfect health. Indeed, after a day or two I began to feel much too well to be a prisoner. Under the desert stars one thought of the lights of London. Perversely, instead of being grateful for the unfettered grandeur of one's surroundings, one thought regretfully of the crowded hours one spends among civilised peoples. And, oh, how tired I was of seeing nothing but men! One of the worst features of captivity is that it is generally a story without a heroine.

After the second day of travel I was really seriously in need of a heroine, for my friend had developed high fever. If only there had been a ministering angel among our party! I did my best, but am not a nurse by nature. My friend grew so weak that he could not stand; and I began to doubt whether he would get to our journey's end.

But although no heroine came to our help, a hero did. As he happens to be a Turk, I will describe him shortly. Let us call him the Boy Scout, for he did (not one, but many) good actions every day. Out of his valise he produced a phial of brandy, tea, sugar, raisins, and some invaluable medicines. All these he pressed us to accept. He even tried to make me believe that he could spare a box of Bir-inji (first-class) cigarettes, until I discovered he had no more for himself. At every halting place he went to search for milk for my friend. Until we had been provided for, he never attended to his own comforts. After eighty miles of travelling everyone is tired, but although the Boy Scout must have been as tired as any of us, for he rode instead of driving, and although he had no official position with regard to us, no brother officer could have been more helpful or more truly kind. From the moment of our meeting we had been attracted by each other. At times, a look or an inflection of voice will proclaim a kindred spirit in a perfect stranger. Something happens above our consciousness; soul speaks to soul perhaps. So it was with the Boy Scout. He was unknown to me when I first saw him, dark-eyed and graceful, riding a white horse like a prince in a fairy book, and we spoke no common language, but somehow we understood each other.

He was a high official, I afterwards heard, travelling incognito, and had been engaged on Intelligence work for his country in Afghanistan. But, although an enemy in theory, he was a friend in fact. The war was far. Here in the desert we met as brothers. A finer figure of a man I have rarely seen, nor a truer gentleman. He was an ardent Young Turk, and if other Young Turks were cast in such a mould, there would be a place in the world for the race of Othman. But I have never seen another like him.

His manners were perfect, and although we discussed every subject under the sun in snatches of French and broken bits of Persian, we always managed to avoid awkward topics such as atrocities, reprisals, and the like. He guessed, I think, that I often thought of escape, and said one day:

"I shall fully understand if you try to get away, but you will forgive me, won't you, if I use my revolver?"

I assured him I would.

"Good!" he laughed, "because I am a dead shot!"

One day we must meet again, and pick up the threads of talk.

At Ress-el-Ain we separated for a time, and my friend was carried into the train, where he lay down and took no further interest in the proceedings. I also lay down, exhausted by anxiety. I was glad to be quit of the desert. Under other conditions it might have been charming, but its glamour is invisible to a captive's eyes.

The train journey was not very interesting, except for the fact that our guard commander (excited perhaps by the approach to civilisation, or else because he was free from the restraining influence of our teetotal Boy Scout) purchased a bottle of *'araq* and imbibed it steadily on the journey between Ress-el-Ain and Djerablisse.

'Araq, the reader must know, is otherwise known as *mastic* or *douzico*, and is a colourless alcohol distilled from raisins and flavoured with aniseed, which clouds on admixture with water, and tastes like cough-mixture. It is an intoxicant without the saving grace of more generous vintages. It inebriates but does not cheer.

At Djerablisse, on the Euphrates, our guard commander supplemented the fiery *'araq* with some equally potent German ration rum. By the time we got to Aleppo next day, he was reeking of this blend of alcohols. Not all the perfumes of Arabia could have stifled its fumes, nor all the waters of Damascus have quenched his thirst. He was besotted.

Escape would have been possible then. We had become separated from the rest of our party and were in charge of one old, sleepy, and rather friendly soldier. There seemed to be some doubt in his mind as to where we should pass the night, but we eventually arrived at a small and clean Turkish hotel, where we were told, rather mysteriously, that we should be among friends.

I looked for friends, but as everyone was asleep, it being then two o'clock in the morning, I decided to have a good night's rest before making any plans. Our dainty bedroom was too tempting to be ignored. The curtains were of Aleppo-work, in broad stripes of black and gold. The rafters were striped in black and white. The walls were dead white, the furniture dead black. Three pillows adorned our beds, of black, and of crimson, and of brilliant blue, each with a white slip covering half their length. The bed-covers were black, worked with gold dragons. It was like a room one imagines in dreams, or sees at the Russian Ballet.

After a blissful night, between sheets, and on a spring mattress, tea was brought to us in bed, and immediately afterwards, as no guards seemed to be about, I rose, greatly refreshed, and dressed in haste. My idea was to order a carriage to drive us to the sea-coast at Mersina, from which place I felt sure it would be possible to charter a boat to Cyprus.

But these hasty plans were dispelled by finding the Boy Scout waiting for me in the passage.

"Your guard commander was ill," he explained, "so I arranged that you should be brought to this hotel, where you are my guests. And I want you to lunch with me at one o'clock."

My face fell, but of course there was no help for it. And the Boy Scout's hospitality was princely indeed.

After delicious hors-d'oeuvres (the *mézé*—as it is called in Turkey—is a national dish) and soup, and savoury meats, we refreshed our palates with bowls of curds and rice. Then we attacked the sweets, which were melting morsels of honey and the lightest pastry. After drinking the health of the invalid (who could not join us of course) in Cyprian wine, we adjourned to the Boy Scout's room for coffee and cigarettes. Here I found all his belongings spread out, including several tins of English bully-beef and slabs of chocolate, which he said was his share of the loot taken after our retirement at the Dardanelles. He begged us to help ourselves to everything we wanted in the way of food or clothing; and he was ready, literally, to give us his last shirt. After having fitted us out, he telephoned to the hospital about the patient, and made arrangements that he should be received that afternoon.

Some hours later, accordingly, I drove to the hospital with my friend, accompanied by two policemen who had arrived from district headquarters, no doubt at the Boy Scout's request.

We were met at the entrance of the hospital by two odd little doctors.

"What is the matter with him?" squeaked Humpty in French.

"Fever," said I.

"Fever, indeed!" answered Dumpty, "let's look at his chest."

"And at his back," added Humpty suspiciously.

My friend disrobed, shivering in the sharp air, and these two strange physicians glared at him, standing two yards away, while the Turkish soldier and I supported the patient.

"He hasn't got it," they said suddenly in chorus.

"Hasn't what?"

"Typhus, of course. Carry him in. He will be well in a week."

I doubted it, but the situation did not admit of argument. We carried him in, through a crowd of miserable men in every stage of disease, all clamouring for admittance. No one, I gathered, was allowed into that hospital merely for the dull business of dying. They could do that as well outside. Thankful for small mercies, therefore, I left my friend in the clutches of Humpty and Dumpty, and even as they had predicted, he was well within a week.

There is something rather marvellous about a Turkish doctor's diagnosis. Such trifles as the state of your temperature or tongue are not considered. They trust in the Lord and give you an emetic. Although unpleasant, their methods are often efficacious.

It was now my turn to fall ill, and I did it with startling suddenness and completeness. I was sitting at the window of the house in which we were confined in Aleppo, feeling perfectly well, when I began to shiver violently. In half an hour I was in a high fever. That night I was taken to Humpty and Dumpty. Next morning I was unconscious.

I will draw a veil over the next month of my life. Only two little incidents are worth recording.

The first occurred about a week after my admittance to hospital, when my disease, whatever it was, had reached its crisis. A diet of emetics is tedious, so also is the companionship of people suffering from *delirium tremens* when one wants to be quiet. An end, I felt, must be made of the present situation. Creeping painfully out of my bed, I went down the passage, holding against the wall for support. It was a dark, uneven passage, with two patches of moonlight from two windows at the far end. Near one of these pools of light I caught my foot in a stone, and slipped and fell. I was too weak to get up again. I cooled my head on the stones and wondered what would happen next. Then I began to think of seas and rivers. All the delightful things I had ever done in water kept flitting through my mind. I remembered crouching in the bow of my father's cat-boat as we beat up a reach to Salem (Massachusetts) with the spray in our faces. And I thought of the sparkling sapphire of the Mediterranean and the cool translucencies of Cuckoo-weir.... No one came to disturb my meditations. The moonlight shifted right across my body, and slowly, slowly, I felt the wells of consciousness were filling up again. I was, quite definitely, coming back to life. It was as if I had really been once more in America and Italy and by the Thames, living again in all memories connected with open waters, and as if their solace had somehow touched me. Their coolness had cured me, and I was now flying back through imperceptible ether to Aleppo. I was coming back to that passage in a Turkish hospital.... .

Did I draw, I wonder, upon some banked reserve of vitality, or were my impressions a common phase of illness? Anyway, when I came to, I was a different man. The waters of the world had cured me.

Later, during the journey to Afion-kara-hissar, I had a relapse. This second incident of my illness was a spiritual experience. Having been carried by my friend to the railway station, I collapsed on the platform, while he was momentarily called away. So dazed and helpless was I that I lay inconspicuously on some sacks, a bundle of skin and bone that might not have been human at all. Some porters threw more sacks on the pile and I was soon almost covered. But I lay quite still: I was too tired to move or to cry out. As bodily weakness increased, so there came to me a sense of mental power, over and beyond my own poor endowments. I thrilled to this strange strength, which seemed to mount to the very throne of Time, where past and future are one. Call it a whimsy of delirium if you will, nevertheless, one of the scenes I saw in the cinema of clairvoyance was a scene that actually happened some three months later, at that same station where I lay... . I saw some hundred men, prisoners from Kut and mostly Indians, gathered on the platform. One of these men was sitting on this very heap of sacks; he was sitting there rocking himself to and fro in great agony, for one of the guards had struck him with a thick stick and broken his arm. But not only was his arm broken, the spirit within him (which I also saw) was shattered beyond repair. No hope in life remained: he had done that which is most terrible to a Hindu, for he had eaten the flesh of cows and broken the ordinances of caste. His companions had died in the desert without the lustral sacrifice of water or of fire, and he would soon die also, a body defiled, to be cast into outer darkness. For a time the terror and the tragedy of that alien brain was mine; I shared its doom and lived its death. Later I learnt that a party of men, coming out of the great tribulation of the desert, had halted at this station, and a Hindu soldier with a broken arm had died on those sacks. I record the incident for what it is worth.

Without my friend I should never have achieved this journey. My gratitude is a private matter, though I state it here, with some mention of my own dull illness, in order to picture in a small way the sufferings of our men from Kut. When some were sick and others hale, the death-rate was not so high, but with many parties, such as those whose ghosts I believe I saw, there was no possibility of helping each other. So starved and so utterly weary were they, that they had no energy beyond their own existence. Many men must have died with no faith left in man or God.

On arrival at Afion-kara-hissar, we were shown into a bare house. For a day I rested blissfully on the floor, asking for nothing better than to be allowed to lie still for ever and ever. But this was not to be. On the second day of our stay we noticed signs of great excitement among our guards. They nailed barbed wire round our windows, and they watched us anxiously through skylights, and counted us continually, as if uncertain whether two and two made four.

Presently the meaning of their precautions was divulged. Some English prisoners had escaped, and our captors were engaged in locking the stable door after the steeds had gone. All the prisoners in Afion-kara-hissar were marshalled in the street, and marched off to the Armenian church, situated at the base of the big rock that dominates the town. Hither we also marched, with our new companions, singing the prisoners' anthem:

> "We *won't* be bothered about
> Wherever we go, we always shout
> We won't be bothered about.... .
> We're bothered if we'll be bothered about!"

greatly to the astonishment of the townsfolk, who connected the Armenian church with massacres rather than melody. The leader of our band was a wounded officer, in pyjamas and a bowler hat (this being the sum of his possessions) who waved his crutch as a conductor's baton. (Alas! his cheery voice is stilled, for he died in hospital a year later. R.I.P.) I can still see him hobbling along—a tall figure in pink pyjamas, with one leg swinging (bandaged to the size of a bolster) and his hat askew, and his long chin stuck out defiantly—hymn-writer and hero *manqué*—fit leader of lost causes and of our fantastic pageant to that church.

It was a gay and motley crew of prisoners of all nationalities and conditions of life who entered its solemn and rather stuffy precincts. We were all delighted to be "strāfed" in a worthy cause. Three good men had escaped, and more might follow later.

To anyone in decent health the month we spent in the Armenian church must have been an interesting experience. Even to me, it was not without amusement. Imagine a plain, rather gloomy, church, built of oak and sandstone, with a marble chancel in the east. Two rooms opened out on either side of the altar, and there was a high gallery in the west. In the body of the building the English camped. One of the small rooms was taken by the French, the other we reserved for a chapel. The Russians chiefly inhabited the space between the chancel and the altar, but the overflow of nationalities mingled. Our soldier servants were put in the gallery. When everyone was fitted in, there was no space to move, except in the centre aisle. There was no place for exercise nor any arrangements for washing or cooking. During our stay in the church two men died of typhus, and it is extraordinary that the infection did not spread, considering the lack of sanitation. During the first night of the strafe, the Russians, accustomed to pogroms in their own country, thought there was a likelihood of being massacred, and kept watch through the small hours of the morning by clumping up and down the aisle in their heavy boots. All night long—for I was sleepless too—I watched these grave, bearded pessimists waiting for a death which did not come, while the French and English slept the sleep of optimists. At last dawn arrived, and lit the windows over the altar, and a few moments later the sunlight crept into the northern transept. Then the Russians gave up their vigil, dropped in their tracks, and at once began snoring in the aisle, like great watch-dogs.

The noise the two hundred of us made in sleeping was remarkable. Probably our nerves were rather queer. The church was never silent through the night. Some cried out continually in their slumbers, others went through a pantomime of eating. Some moaned, others chuckled. One sleeper gave a hideous laugh at intervals. One could hear it deep down in his throat, and mark it gradually bubbling to his lips until he grew vocal like some horrible hyena. But it is small wonder that the prisoners in the church were restless. The marvel is that they slept at all. Nearly all of us had lived through trying moments, and had felt the hand of Providence, whose power makes one tremble. We knew the shivers of retrospection. One officer, for instance, wounded in an attack on Gallipoli, had been dragged as a supposed corpse to the Turkish trenches and there built into the parapet. But he was none the worse now for his amazing experiences, except that he suffered slightly from deafness, as his neck had formed the base of a loophole. Then there was a man, left as dead after an attack, who recovered consciousness but not the use of his limbs, and lay helpless in the path of the Turkish retreat. For an hour the passers-by prodded him with bayonets, so that he now has twenty-seven wounds and a large gap in his body where there should be solid flesh. From the very brink of the valley of the shadow this boy of nineteen had returned to life. Again, there was a young Frenchman, who lay four days and nights between the lines, dying of the twin tortures of thirst and a stomach wound; but by a miracle he survived, and now at night, sometimes, when will lost its grip on consciousness, he would live those ninety-six hours again. Then there were the submarine crews, out of the jaws of the worst death conceivable. One crew had lived for a whole day struggling in a net at the bottom of the Dardanelles while the air became foul and hope waned, and the submarine "sweated," and depth charges exploded so close to them that on one occasion the shock knocked a teapot off a table! Hemmed in and helpless, the clammy agony of that suspense might well haunt their sleeping hours.

But on the whole our psychology was normal. Only, at nights, if one lay awake, did one realise the stress and stark horror through which the sleepers had lived. Out of four hundred officers "missing" at the Dardanelles, only some forty were surviving at Afion-kara-hissar. This fact speaks for itself.

By day we wandered about, so far as the congestion permitted, making friends and exchanging experiences. To us, lately from Mesopotamia, the then unknown story of Gallipoli stirred our blood as it will stir the blood of later men.

I ate and drank the anecdotes of Gallipoli as they were told me. I loved the hearing of them, in the various dialects of the protagonists, from a lordly lisp to a backwood burr. The brogue, the northern drawl, the London twang, the elided g's or the uncertain h's, had each their several and distinct fascination. There is joy in hearing one's own tongue again after a time of strange speech and foreign faces.

> "Beyond our reason's sway,
> Clay of the pit whence we were wrought
> Yearns to its fellow-clay."

The many voices of the many British were better than sweet music.

But we had plenty of sweet music as well. The sailors amongst us were the cheeriest crew imaginable.

A résumé of our life at that time would be that we sang often about nothing in particular, swore continually at life in general, smoked heavily, gambled mildly, and drank *'araq* when we could get it, and tea when we couldn't. Not everyone, I hasten to add, did all these things. As in everyday life, there were some who said that the constant cigarette was evil, and that cards were a curse, and drink the devil. But, again, as in everyday life, their example had no effect on cheerful sinners.

> "Here's to the bold and gallant three
> Who broke their bonds and sought the sea"

sang one of the poets of our captivity, and all of us French, Russians, and English, took up the chorus with a roar. The Turkish sentries protested vainly, and some, ostentatiously loading their rifles, went up to the Western gallery which overlooked the body of the church. As we were being treated like Armenians, they could not understand why we did not behave like Armenians and herd silently together, as sheep before a storm. Instead, two hundred lusty voices proclaimed to anyone who cared to listen that we were not downhearted.

See us then at midnight, seated at a table under the high altar. About fifty of us are celebrating somebody's birthday, and a demi-john of *'araq* graces the festive board. We have sung every song we know, and many we don't.

> "Jolly good song and jolly well sung,
> Jolly good fellows every one... .
> Wow! Wow!"

The chorus dies down, and the Master of the Ceremonies, still in pyjamas and bowler hat, rises on his sound leg and standing (swaying slightly) at the head of the table, raps on it with his crutch for silence.

One officer wears a soup-bowl for a Hun helmet. Others are dressed as parodies of Turks, and have been acting in a farce entitled "The Escape." Two Irish friends of mine are singing "The Wearing of the Green," while others are patriotically drowning their voices. A submarine skipper, with a mane of yellow hair over his face, like a lion in a picture-book, watches a diplomat dancing a horn-pipe. A little bald flying man of gigantic strength and brain, is wrestling with a bearded Hercules. Some sailors are singing an old sea-chanty.

The rough deal table, littered with pipes and glasses, the tallow-dips lighting the vaulted gloom, the bearded roysterers singing songs older than Elizabeth's time, the simple fare of bread and meat, the simpler jokes and horseplay, took one back through centuries to other men who made the best of war. In Falstaff's time such scenes as these must have passed in the taverns of Merrie England. Only here, there were no wenches to serve us with sack. We had to mix our own *'araq*.

"Silence, if you please," says he of the long jowl, using his crutch as a chairman's hammer. "Silence for the prisoners' band."

The band begins. It consists of penny whistles, banjos, castanets, soup-bowls, knives and forks, and anything else within reach. The *motif* of the piece is our release. *Andante con coraggio* we pass the weary months ahead. Then the dawn of our liberation breaks. We smash everything we possess, while the train to take us away steams into the station.

Sh! Shh! Shhh! Chk! Chk! Chk! Bang! Swish!! We take our seats amid a perfect pandemonium. Then the train whistles—louder and louder—and we move off—faster and faster and faster and *faster*, until no one can make any more noise, and the dust of our stamping has risen like incense to the roof, in a grand finale of freedom.

Strange doings in a church, you say? But what would you? We had nowhere else to go. There is a time for everything after all, and it is a poor heart that never rejoices. I feel sure Solomon himself would have sung with us, and proved most excellent company.

On Sunday mornings Divine Service was always well attended. Perhaps by contrast with my usual methods of passing the time, those Sabbath hours are set as so many jewels in the tarnished shield of idleness. The fadeless beauty of our Common Prayer brought hope and consolation to all of us who were gathered together. We repeated the grand old words; we sang "Fight the Good Fight" and "Onward, Christian Soldiers." We shared then, however humbly, in the tears and triumph of our cause. We were not of that white company that was to die for England, but we could share the sorrow of the women who mourned, and of the old who stood so sadly outside the fray.

And as through a magic door, I passed from that barren room to a country church where the litany for all prisoners and captives went up to Heaven, mingled with the fragrance of English roses.

CHAPTER V

THE LONG DESCENT OF WASTED DAYS

Afion-kara-hissar means "Black Opium Rock" in Turkish, but it is not as interesting a place as it sounds. The only romantic visitors are the storks, who use it as an aerodrome on their bi-annual migrations. They blacken the sky when they come, in flights a thousand strong, swooping and circling over the plain and alighting finally near the black rocks that give the town its name. With one leg tucked up, and pensive beak back-turned, they form arresting silhouettes against the sunset. And curiously enough, the Turkish children know that they bring babies to the home.

We lived in four cottages, connected by a common garden. They were quite new—so new that they had no windows or conveniences. We fitted frames and panes, we erected bathrooms, installed kitchen ranges, made beds out of planks and string, and tables out of packing-cases. We made everything, in fact, except the actual houses.

I daresay that at this time we were better treated than the officer prisoners in Germany. Not so the men. We officers had plenty to eat, though it cost a great deal, but the men were always half starved when for any reason they could not supplement their ration from Ambassador's money, or private remittances from home. Every month the American (and later the Dutch) Embassy used to send a sum of money to our prisoners to help them buy something more nourishing than the black bread and soup provided by the Turks. When this relief did not arrive in time, or the Turks delayed in distributing it, our men suffered the greatest hardship. Treatment in Turkey was all a question of money. The officers could, and did, cash cheques while in captivity, and were able to pay for the necessities (and sometimes also the minor luxuries) of existence, but the men were entirely dependent on what was given them. Although some had bank balances, no one except an officer was allowed to write a cheque.

Here it is fitting to say a word in praise of those organisations who sent out parcels to our prisoners. No words can express our gratitude to them. To us officers, parcels were sometimes in the nature of a luxury, though none the less welcome. But to the men, who starved in dungeons of the interior, they came as a very present help in time of need. The prisoners' parcels saved many lives, and I hope the kind people who worked so hard at home against all sorts of difficulties and disappointments realise how grateful we are, and what a great work they did. Besides the material relief of provisions, the moral effect of a parcel from home on the mind of a sick prisoner cannot be over estimated. To open something packed by English hands was like a breath of home to him.

We were allowed no communication with the men, so it was very difficult to help them. Whether the worst done to our prisoners in Germany equals the worst in Turkey I do not know. To compare two horrors is profitless. But I do know something of the sufferings of our men, and when I write of my own petty amusements and comedies of captivity I do not for a moment forget the tragedy of their lives.

Light and shade, however, there must be in every picture, else it is not a picture at all. And there must be colour in the canvas, however grim the subject.

The poppy fields, which give the town the first part of its name,[1] lay right underneath our windows, across the station road. In June, when they were white with blossom, and the farmers' wives came out to drain the precious fluid from the buds, I used to gaze and gaze at the beauty of the world, and long for freedom. To be cooped up in a little room when the world was green and white, and the sky a flawless blue, and summer rode across the open lands, was miserable. It was unbearable to be growing old and immobile, like the hills on the horizon, when one might be out among the poppy blossoms. Of what use to be alive, if one did not share in the youth of the world?

But we were closely guarded in our cottages and rarely allowed out, except into the back garden—a bare space some hundred yards by thirty, which was the scene of most of our small activities, from early morning skipping to the mid-day display of our washing, and from the occasional amateur theatricals of an evening to the rare but tense moments of an attempted escape.

A diary of my days might run as follows:

Monday. Up at 6 a.m. Skipped 200 times. Two eggs for breakfast, tried my new *pekmes*.[2] Read *Hilal*.[3] Looked out places on my hidden map. Long argument about the use of cavalry in modern war. Walk in garden. Mutton cutlets for lunch. Completed my new hammock. Argued about Free Trade. Played badminton in garden. Read philosophy with —— and ——. *Sakuska*[4] party with —— and —— at 7.30. Watched Polly picking opium. Dinner at 8. Soup, eggs, suet; very satisfactory. Bridge and bed.

Tuesday. Up at 6.15. Skipped 250 times, and had a boxing lesson. Painful. Two eggs for breakfast, but one bad. *Hilal* did not arrive. Argued about yesterday's cavalry news. Walk in garden. No meat for lunch. Bitten by mosquitoes in my hammock. Argued about Protection. Ran round the garden ten times. My wind is getting worse. *Sakuska* party at sevenish with —— and —— in my room. Polly was seen out walking with a *posta*.[5] Dinner at 8. Mutton cutlets. Chess and bed.

And so on, *ad infinitum.*

I had at that time come to the conclusion that I could not reach the coast from Afion-kara-hissar, so for some time I sought a mental rather than a physical escape from my surroundings. Philosophy seemed an ideal subject under the circumstances, and in the company of two friends of like mind, I made some study of "Creative Evolution." Every afternoon we used to forgather for tea, in a little room I had built, where our joint contributions provided a well-selected pabulum of cakes and jam and Bergson, so that the inner and the outer man were Platonically at one. But to plunge from *le tremplin de la vie* is not easy in captivity. Lack of employment cripples imagination. The average mind works best when it has practical things to do, and mine, such as it is, boggles at abstractions more quickly than it tires of talk.

When this occurred the best thing to do was to laugh. A friend and I used to laugh for hours sometimes over weak and washy stories that would hardly pass muster, even in the small hours of the morning. But they did us good. Generally, however, the time between tea and dinner was spent in learned and weighty discussions on appearance, reality, and the problems of Being and Not-being.

With my two friends

> "... the seed of Wisdom did I sow
> And with my own Hand arboured it to grow,
> But this was all the Harvest that I reaped—
> I came like Water and like Wind I go."

Only unfortunately I did not go. I remained firmly at Afion-kara-hissar. When philosophy failed me, the hours spent in planning escapes and concocting cyphers were those which passed most easily. But the craft of cyphers, interesting though it be, cannot be discussed in print. Like the preparation of poisons, it must remain part of the unpublished knowledge of the world, until the millennium. As regards escapes, some of us thought a great deal, and did very little. There were, however, some ingenious attempts made to get to Constantinople. One officer conceived the idea of going there to be treated for hydrophobia, and, after inflicting suitable wounds in the calf of his leg with a pair of nail scissors, he asserted that a certain dog, well known in the camp, had exhibited strange symptoms of insanity, amongst others, that of suddenly biting him in the leg. This ruse would have succeeded but for the fact that the Turks did not treat hydrophobia with any seriousness. Kismet takes no account of the Pasteur system. Short of actually snapping at someone, the officer could not have established a belief in his infection. He found it simpler to feign another ailment. Two other officers, however, of a still more picturesque turn of mind, declared that they themselves were mad, and actually hung themselves as a proof of insanity. They were found one morning by their astonished sentries suspended from a rafter, and apparently in the last stages of strangulation. Convinced that they were "afflicted of God," the Turks sent them to hospital, and carefully watched for any symptoms of suicidal mania. After various astonishing experiences, in their rôle of madmen, amongst real madmen in a Turkish lunatic ward, they were eventually exchanged.

In sheer manual dexterity, our prisoners also showed great resource. The soldiers who were employed on making a tunnel through the Taurus, to take one example, succeeded in purloining various odds and ends from the workshops where they laboured under German supervision, until they eventually were able to build for themselves a complete collapsible boat. This boat they actually tested at dead of night on a river near their camp, before setting out to reach the coast. That success did not crown their efforts was sheer bad luck. Luck, also, was against most of the forty officers who concerted a simultaneous escape from Yuzgad, and prepared for it in absolute secrecy, down to the smallest detail, for months beforehand. Some of them even made their own boots. Only eight out of the original party actually got out of the country, however. Their story, surely one of the most remarkable ever written, has recently been published.

The two great difficulties in any attempt to escape were: firstly, that the Turks, by spies or otherwise, studied the psychology of every individual prisoner, setting special guards on the more enterprising among them, and, secondly, that the distance of the camp from the coast, and the number of brigands infesting every mile of that distance, was such that it was extremely difficult to gain the sea, let alone embark upon it.

The spies made some very bad guesses about the intentions of the prisoners. One harmless and elderly officer was seen greasing a pair of marching boots, and this gave rise to the most sinister suspicions. Where could the officer want to march to, except the coast? He was immediately asked for his parole, and gave it.

Exercise in any form was a sign of incipient madness in the eyes of the Turks. Why, they argued, should anyone in his right mind skip five hundred times, and then splash himself with ice-cold water? If he did such things, he ought certainly to be placed under restraint. Boxing, again, was a suspect symptom. A man who bled at the nose for pleasure might commit any enormity. In order to circumvent suspicion it was necessary to adopt the utmost caution. The method I myself employed is described in a later chapter. One friend of mine, while training for a trip to Blighty, habitually carried heavy lead plates hung round his waist, to accustom himself to the weight of his pack. Such were the internal difficulties. But outside the camp the problems were even more puzzling. How to avoid the brigands—how to carry food enough for the journey—how to elude our guards and get a few hours' start—what clothes to wear and what pack to carry—how to find one's way—how to get a boat once the coast was reached—here were well-nigh insoluble questions, which provided, however, excellent topics for talk.

I talked about these things for eighteen months. But I will ask the reader to skip that dismal procession of moons, and come directly to the day when I was asked by the Commandant to sign a paper stating that I would not attempt to escape. I naturally refused, as also did another officer to whom the same request was made.

Our negotiations in this matter, while interesting to us at the time, and involving the composition of several noble documents in French, led to the sad result that we were both transferred, at an hour's notice, to a little box of a house in the Armenian quarter. Once inside the house, with the various belongings we had collected during a twelve-month of captivity in Afion-kara-hissar, we two completely filled the only habitable room. And although habitable in a sense, this room was already occupied by undesirable tenants.

I must here, rather diffidently, introduce the subject of vermin. But, saving the public's presence, bugs are the very devil. Other insects are nothing to them. Lice the gallant reader may have met at the front. Fleas are a common experience. Centipedes and scorpions are well known in India. But bugs are Beelzebub's especial pets, and Beelzebub is a ruler in Turkey. It is quite impossible to write of my captivity there without mentioning these small, flat creatures who live in beds. I cannot disregard them: they have bitten into my very being.

Imagine lying down, after a sordid day of dust and disagreeableness. One thinks of home, or the sea. One tries to slide out to the gulfs of sleep, where healing is. But rest does not come: there is a sense of malaise. One's skin feels irritable and unclean. Presently there is an itching at one's wrists, and at the back of one's neck. One squashes something, and there is a smear of blood (one's own good blood) and one realises that one's skin (one's own good skin) is being punctured by these evil beasts. Almost instantly one squashes another. A horrible odour arises. One lights the candle, and there, scuttling under the pillow, are five or six more of these loathsome vermin. They not only suck one's blood. They sap one's faith in life.

> "If one could dream that such a world began
> In some slow devil's heart that hated man,"

indeed one would not be mistaken. In them the powers of Satan seem incarnate.

Having killed every bug in sight, one lies back and gasps. And then, out of the corner of one's eye, creeping up the pillow, and hugely magnified by proximity, another monstrous brute appears. It runs forward, horribly avid, and eager, and brisk. All the cruelty of nature is in its hideous head, all the activity of evil in its darting body. Presently another and another appear. There is no end to them. You kill them on the bed, and they appear on the walls. You search out and slaughter every form of life within reach, but the bugs still drop on you from the ceiling. No killing can assuage their appetite for a healthy body. Reckless of danger, they batten on the young. Regardless of death, they swarm to silky skin. Of two victims, they will always choose the one in best condition.

After being eaten by bugs for some time, one feels infected with their contamination. It is almost impossible to rise superior to them. In one night a man can live through the miseries of Job.

It may be imagined therefore that our confinement in that little house was not amusing. My companion in misfortune and myself lived in that box for a week with the bugs, without once going out of the door. Now, to stay in a room for a week may not seem a very trying punishment (I was later to spend a month in solitary confinement); but when the punishment is wholly undeserved, and when, moreover, one is wrongly suspected of something one would like to do but has not done, and when one is bitten all night, and when from confinement one sees other officers walking about in comparative freedom, one naturally begins to fret.

There were compensations, however. Firstly, a friendship grew between my companion and myself which I hope will endure through life. Secondly, as a prisoner, any sort of change is welcome. And, thirdly, we felt we were doing something useful. The Commandant did not dare to force us to sign parole. Neither could he keep us permanently in special restraint. It is rarely that one gets the chance, as a prisoner, of putting the enemy on the horns of such a dilemma.

This Commandant, an ugly, drunken beast, who is now, I hope, expiating the innumerable crimes he committed against our men, caused a search to be made one day amongst the effects of all the prisoners at Afion-kara-hissar. One of the most interesting things he found was a diary kept by a senior British officer, with the following entry:

"New Commandant arrived. His face looks as if it was meant to strike matches on."

No better description could possibly have been written. He was a vain man, and it must have cut him to the quick to see himself as others saw him.

After a month of "special treatment" the Commandant learnt that Turkish Army Headquarters, fearing reprisals, no doubt, would not support his bluff in punishing us if we did not give parole. He had to climb down completely.

We were transferred to another house, in the Armenian quarter, already occupied by some R.N.A.S. officers, who were all determined to escape if opportunity arose. A very cheery house-party we made.

The time was now the year of grace 1917, and our life was organised to some extent. Once or twice a week we were allowed to play football, or go for a walk. On Thursdays we used to troop down in a body to visit the officers in the other houses, and on Monday mornings we were sometimes able, with special permission, to attend the weekly fair of coke and firewood held in the market-place. All this gave an interest to our lives, and money, so long as one was prepared to write cheques, was not a source of difficulty. The Turks, in fact, encouraged us to write cheques, exchanging them for Turkish notes at nearly double their face value (190 piastres for a pound was the best I myself received), because they rightly thought that our signature was worth more than the guarantees of the Turkish Government. I heard afterwards that our cheques had a brisk circulation on the Constantinople Bourse. But one was loth to write many. Five pounds is five pounds—and in Turkey it represented only a packet of tea or a kilogram of sugar... . I saved as much as I could for bribes when escaping.

A microscopic, but not unamusing, social life was in full swing. There were parties and politics, clubs and cliques. Each prisoner, according to his temperament, took his choice between grave pursuits and gay.

There were lecturers (really good ones) who discoursed on a wide range of topics, from Mendelism to Mesopotamia. There were professors of French, Italian, Greek, Russian, Turkish, Arabic, Hindustani, and I daresay all the languages of Babel, ready to teach in return for reciprocal instruction in English. Our library contained many luminous volumes, kindly sent out by the Board of Trade. Law and Seamanship, Semaphoring and Theology, Carpentry and the Integral Calculus, Gardening and Genetics—such is a random selection of the subjects on which there were experts available and eager to impart information.

But, personally, my mind resisted the seductions of learning. I learned only how to waste time. And sometimes, perhaps, I touched the hem of

Philosophy's garment, and stammered a few words to her. Otherwise I did nothing except try to forget things … things seen.

Yet one enjoyed oneself, occasionally. The football was great fun. So also were some of the lighter sides of our indoor life. Poker used to pass the time. So also, though more rarely, did reading. The plays which a dramatist—soon to be eminent, I expect—presented to enthusiastic audiences are delightful memories. His revues and topical verses were worthy of a wider audience, and I am sure his work—unlike the most of our labours—will not be wasted.

But best of all, I think, was to sit in a circle on the floor round a brazier on a winter's evening, and sip hot lemon *'araq*, and listen to songs and stories. It was a relief to laugh, and forget the fate of those we could not help.

> "Sweet life, if love were stronger,
> Earth clear of years that wrong her…"

sang a soft Irish voice, whose melody seemed to melt into the cold of one's captivity…. . Then there were the fancy dress balls held on New Year's Eve in 1917 and 1918. So good were they that for the night one completely forgot one's surroundings. A very attractive barmaid dispensed refreshments behind a table. There were several debutantes, and at least one chaperone. Pierrot was there, and Pierrette, and Mephistopheles, and Bacchus, and a very realistic Pirate. If some reveller in London had looked in on us at midnight he might easily have fancied himself at an Albert Hall dance. He would certainly not have guessed that all the clothes and furniture and food were home-made, and that everyone in the room was a British officer. The self-confident flapper, for instance, who could only have given him "the next missing three" was a Major in the Flying Corps. And the girl at the bar, with big brown eyes, who would have offered him *'araq* so charmingly was really a submarine officer of the Navy, and a well-known figure at "The Goat."

After functions such as these, the morning after the night before found me wondering where it would all end. If the war lasted another ten years, would I ever be fit to take a place in normal life? How long could I keep sane in this topsy-turvy world? …

The weather in the winter of 1918 was absolutely arctic. For a month there was a very hard frost, and during all this time, had it not been for festivities such as the foregoing I should have stayed stupidly in bed and hibernated until the spring. Intenser cold I have never felt. In the room in which we dined the water froze in our glasses on several occasions while we were eating our evening meal. Icy winds howled through the house, and the paper windows we had improvised (to replace unobtainable glass) had burst, through weight of snow. Also, the plaster of the outer walls of our mansion had peeled off, so that cold blasts penetrated through the walls. With few clothes and only one pair of leaky boots it was impossible to keep warm and dry-shod. Fuel, of course, was very scarce. In my bedroom some precious quarts of beer, which I was preserving for Christmas, froze and cracked their bottles. I invited a party to taste my blocks of amber ice, but they were better to look at than to swallow.

Under these climatic conditions washing was a labour that took one the best part of the morning, and until I caught a chill I used to economize time and fuel by rolling in the snow on the flat roof of my house. This amused me, and surprised the neighbourhood, but it was a poor substitute for a bath. That winter was a black, bleak time.

During the hard frost it was impossible to escape, but we used occasionally to reconnoitre the sentries outside our house after lock-up. I have spent some amusing moments in this way, especially in watching one sentry (generally on duty at midnight) who used to warm himself by playing with a cat. With pussy on one arm and his rifle on the other, he formed a delightfully casual figure. It would have been quite easy to pass him, but the difficulties lay beyond... .

I then thought, wrongly I dare say, that the only reasonable hope of success lay in starting from Constantinople, and it was to this end that my real schemes were shaping. But I thought it well to have two strings to my bow, and besides, I considered no day well spent which did not include some practical effort towards escape.

A complex of causes contributed to this idea, which became almost an obsession. First, I dare say, was boredom. Second, the feeling that one was not earning one's pay or doing one's duty by remaining idly a prisoner. And thirdly—or was it firstly?—the condition under which our men were living and the crimes which had been committed against them made it imperative that someone should get to England with our news. It was high time, and past high time, that the civilised world should know how our prisoners fared.

I have already written the savage story of our life at Mosul, where the men died from calculated cruelty. The history of the Kut prisoners is even worse, for the crime was on a greater scale.

That garrison, debilitated from the long siege and the climatic conditions of Mesopotamia, were marched right across Asia Minor with hardly any clothes, no money, and insufficient food. Their nameless sufferings will never be known in full, for many died in the desert, clubbed to death by their guards, stripped naked, and left by the roadside. Others were abandoned in Arab villages, when in the last stages of fever or dysentery. Others, more fortunate, were found dead by their companions after the night's halt, when the huddled sleepers turned out to face another day of misery. Hopeless indeed the outlook must have seemed to some lad fresh from the fields of home. The brutal sentries, the arid desert, the daily deaths, the daily quarrels, the bitterness of the future, as bleak as the acres of sand that stretched to their unknown destination, the dwindling company of friends, the grip of thirst, the pangs of hunger, and the pains of death—such was the outlook for many a lad who died between Baghdad and Aleppo. Ghosts of such memories must not be lightly evoked amongst those alive to-day, friends of the fallen, but always they will haunt the trails of the northern Arabian desert.

Through it all our men were heroes. To the last they showed their captors of what stuff the Anglo-Saxon is made. The cowardly Kurds, who were the worst of the various escorts provided between Baghdad and Aleppo, never dared to insult our men unless they outnumbered them four to one. Even then they generally waited until some sick man fell down from exhaustion before clubbing him to death with their rifle-butts.

In the middle of the desert, between Mosul and Aleppo, a friend of mine found six half-demented British soldiers who had been propped up against the wall of a mud hut and left there to die. There was no transport, no medicines. Nothing could be done for them. They died long before the relief parties organised at Aleppo could come to their rescue.

At Aleppo the hospital treatment was extremely bad.

All men who were fit to move (and many who were not) were sent on in cattle trucks to various camps in the centre of Anatolia, and when at length they reached these camps after vicissitudes which were only a dreary repetition of earlier experiences, they came upon the plague of typhus at its height, and naturally, in this weakened state, succumbed by scores and hundreds.

To see a body of our soldiers arriving at Afion-kara-hissar, pushed and kicked and beaten by their escort, was terrible.

Our men were literally skeletons alive, skeletons with skin stretched across their bones, and a few rags on their backs. This is an exact statement of things seen. They struggled up the road, hardly able to carry the pitiful little bundles containing scraps of bread, a bit of soap, a mug, all, in short, that they had been able to save from systematic looting on the way.

In silence, and unswerving, they passed up that road to the hospital, and all who saw those companies of Englishmen so grim and gallant in adversity must have felt proud their veins carried the same blood.

Once in hospital our prisoners fared no better. There were no beds for them, and hardly any blankets or medicines. They died in groups, lying outside the hospital.

It was a common sight to see sad parties of our men passing down this same road, away from the hospital this time, and towards the cemetery. Those weary processions, consisting of four or five emaciated men, with a stretcher and a couple of shovels, used to pass underneath our windows going to bury their comrade. They were a party of skeletons alive, carrying a skeleton dead.

[1] Afion = opium.

[2] *Pekmes*: a substitute for jam and sugar, made from raisins.

[3] The *Hilal*: a Moslem morning paper, published in French.

[4] *Sakuska*: Russian for hors d'oeuvres—such as sardines, frogs' legs, onions, bits of cheese, or indeed anything edible.

[5] *Posta*: a Turkish sentry.

CHAPTER VI

THE PSYCHOLOGY OF PRISON

The contrast of tragedy and farce and the incidents, and the lack of incident, which I have attempted to sketch in the foregoing chapter, had a marked mental effect on all of us. But each felt the effects of confinement differently. With me, I came to look on my life in Turkey as something outside the actuality of existence. I did not feel "myself" at all. I was disembodied, left with no link with the outer world, except memory and anticipation. I was in a dark forest far from all avenues of activity such as the sanity of society and the companionship of women. My world seemed make-believe, and my interests counterfeit.

I worked at a novel with a friend of mine, and for a time that seemed something practical to do. But there was always the fear that it would be taken from us by the Turks, and the possibility that we would never publish it.

Doubt and indecision lay heavy on me. I did not know how long captivity would last. A criminal's sentence is fixed: not so a prisoner of war's. He is dependent on matters beyond his control, and a will beyond his narrow ambit. To reach that outside will, and to form a part of it again, was my dominating wish. Through the glasses of captivity the world was colourless and distorted. Only freedom could make me see it again aright. And when freedom seemed remote, the world was very colourless.

The novel amused me by snatches. Learning languages amused me at times. But these things were really the diversions of a child, who dreams through all its lesson-time of another and a fairer world.

But, unlike a child, I became absorbed in self. I analysed my moods, and thought gloomily about my health. I mourned my youth, as my hair turned grey. The sorrows of the spinster were mine and the griefs of the middle-aged. The value of material things was magnified. The pleasures of the palate, I confess, assumed an exaggerated importance. I found a new joy in food, and sometimes I dreamed that I was eating. Also I contracted the habit of smoking cigarettes in the middle of the night. And I learnt that the effect of alcohol, when one is very depressed, is like putting in the top clutch of the car of consciousness, so that one runs forward smoothly on the road of life. In short, I enjoyed eating and drinking and smoking in a way that I had never done before, and never will again, I hope. But I know now why public-houses flourish. After my own experience of deathly dullness, I heartily sympathise with those who seek relief in alcohol and nicotine. They may be poison, but in this imperfect world the deadliest poison of all is boredom. Prohibition, as I saw it in Turkey, when tobacco was short, or food was scarce, or alcohol was forbidden, did not impress me as being beneficial. The fact is, we all need stimulant of one sort or another. Normally our work, our home, or our hopes supply this need. Almost everyone in the world is struggling (however carefully they may disguise the fact) to be other than they are, and better (or worse) than they are. We strive after superlatives and are rarely satisfied by them. But in captivity, as in other circumstances of distress, this stay in life, this hope of something different and wish for something *more*, is suddenly removed. We are left without *stimuli*. Nothing seems to matter. One's mental and material habits inevitably relax. A muddy idea seems as good as a clear one—a sloppy suit of clothes serves as well as a tidy one. Energy wanes.

But why? The reason is that the average mind cannot live on abstractions. It must grapple with something practical. One must sharpen one's wits on the world, and it is just this that as a prisoner one cannot do. One cannot "lay hold on life," because there is no life to lay hold of, except an unnatural and artificial existence, where the sympathy of women and the dignity of work are absent. That was the crux of the matter. Sympathy and dignity were lacking in our life. We heard of advances and retreats as from another sphere. We read of great heroisms and great sorrows without being close to them. We had no part in the quarrel. We were in a squalid by-way, living out a mean tragedy, while the fate of all we loved was in the balance. Never again would we go fighting.

From the moment of our capture we had passed into a strange narrow life, where the spirit of man, while retaining all its old memories and hopes, could not express them in action.

Captivity is a minor form of death, and I was dead, to all intents and purposes.

Often, lying a-bed in the early morning, I used to feel that my body was completely gone, and that only a fanciful and feverish intelligence remained. I remember especially one dawn in the spring of 1917, when I watched two figures passing down the station road. Slouching towards the station, and all unconscious of the beauty of the waking world, came a soldier with his pack and rifle. He wore the grey Turkish uniform, his beard was grey, his cheeks were also grey and sunken. Slowly, slowly he dragged his heavy feet towards the train that would take him away to the war. The train had been already signalled, I knew (for I kept notes of the traffic in those days), and I found myself hoping anxiously that he would not be late. The sooner he was killed the better. He was old and ugly and ill. If only such as he could perish.... Then my thought took wings of the morning. From the soldier, plodding onwards devotedly, as so many men have gone to their deaths, my eye ranged across the plains, lying dim and dark to eastward, to the horizon mountains of the Suleiman Dagh, whose snow had already seen the messengers of morning hasting from the lands below our world. And man seemed mean and minute in the purposes of Nature. So ugly was he, such a blot on the landscape with his trains and soldiers, that I wondered he continued to exist. There was a life above our life in the dawn. The powers of the world knew nothing of this soldier's hopes and fears. To them his endeavours were a comedy. A huge mountain-back, with the gesture of some giant in the playtime of long ago, seemed shrugging its shoulders at this ridiculous straying atom of a moment's space. The train came in, and I saw its smoke above the tree-tops of the station. It whistled shrilly, and the soldier quickened his pace. No doubt he was late. Perhaps he still survives, and is toiling even now towards some trench. Anyway he passed from my ken, but I still stood at the window, looking towards the mountains and the sky.

Then there passed an archaic ox-cart, creaking down the road slowly, as it has creaked down the ages, from the night of Time. It was drawn by a white heifer, whose shoulders strained against the yoke, for it was a heavy cart. But she went forward willingly, resignedly. Work was her portion. She would live and die under the yoke. She licked her cool muzzle, dusted flies with her neat tail, and looked forward with wistful eyes that seemed to see beyond her working world, to some ultimate haven for the quiet workers. Somewhere she would find rest at last. To my feverish imagination that white heifer symbolised the pathos of all the driven souls who go forward unquestioning to destiny.

And the soldier with his pack was a type also of voiceless millions who carry the burden of our civilisation.

We stagger on, under the bludgeonings of chance, and but rarely lift our eyes to the dawn, although a daily miracle is there. Someone conducts the orient-rite, regardless of the lives of men, which come sweeping on, on the tide of war, to end in foam and froth. Yet from this stir of hate and heroism some purpose must surely rise. From the travail of the trenches some meaning will be born.

I saw things thus, through images and symbols. Across the vast inanity of that waiting time, streaks of vision used to flash, like distant summer lightning. Impermanent, but beautiful to me, they lit a fair horizon. Else, all was dark.

To call this time a death in life seems an overstatement, but if my experiences in Turkey had any mental value at all, it was just this: to teach me how to die. A curtain had come down on consciousness when I was captured. Since then I only lived in the Before and After of captivity. My old self was finished. I saw it in clear but disjunct pictures of recollection: pig-sticking, sailing, dining, dancing, or on the road to Messines one hard November night when feet froze in stirrups and horses slipped and struck blue lights from the cobbles. And my new self awaited the moment of freedom. It still stirred in the womb of war.

Even so, in my belief, do the souls of our comrades lost consider their lives on earth and look back on their time of trial with interest and regret. Discarnate, they cannot achieve their desires, yet they long to manifest again in the world of men. With level and unclouded eyes they consider the incidents of mortality, and find in them a Purpose to continue. There is work for them in the world through many lives, and love, which will meet and re-meet its love. And so at last, drawn by duty and affection, those who have woven their lives in the tapestry of our time will one day take up the threads again.

CHAPTER VII

THE COMIC HOSPITAL IN CONSTANTINOPLE

The one bulwark against morbidity was hope of an escape. Only by getting away, or at any rate making an attempt, could I justify my continued existence, when so many good men were dying in the world outside—and at our own doors.

Now certain spies, as I have told, were constantly on the look-out for officers likely to give trouble to our custodians. The Commandant, I knew, suspected me of wanting to escape, owing to my general eagerness for exercise. I thought, therefore, that if I could induce him to believe that I was ready to dream away my days at Afion-kara-hissar, I should have established that confidence in my character which is the basis of all success. I consequently purchased some two pounds of a certain dark and viscous drug, wrapped in a cabbage leaf. With a sort of theatrical secrecy (for even in Turkey Mrs. Grundy has her say), I proceeded to prepare the stuff by boiling it for two hours in a copper saucepan. I did this on a day when one of the Turkish staff came to the house to distribute letters. Naturally the smell attracted notice. I made flimsy excuses to account for it.

After distilling the decoction, filtering, and then boiling it down to the consistency of treacle, the first phase of my little plan was ended. One of the Turkish staff, a certain Cypriote youth, had become thoroughly interested in my proceedings.

I showed him, under vows of secrecy which I knew he would not keep, the stage property I had bought, consisting of two bamboo pipes, a lamp, a terra-cotta bowl, some darning needles, and the "treacle" in a jampot. Fortunately the most of these implements I had obtained second-hand from a real opium-smoker, so that they did not look too new. Also I had read de Quincey and Claude Farrère. After discussing the subject at length, the Cypriote suggested that we might smoke together one evening. I agreed with alacrity.

One night after lock-up, therefore, I slipped out of my house, with my paraphernalia hidden under my overcoat. A specially bribed Turkish sentry brought me to a silent, shuttered house in a side street. Here the door was opened by an evil-looking harridan, who showed me upstairs to a thickly carpeted room, strewn with cushions, on which my host was lying. The blinds were drawn and only the glimmer of a little green lamp lit the wreaths of whitish smoke which curled down from the low ceiling. The fumes stang my palate and thrilled me with expectancy. I could taste, rather than smell, that strange savour of opium which fascinates its devotees.

I lay down, in the semi-darkness, on a sofa beside my host. After some general conversation, I showed him my pipes and needles, but he said that for that evening I should only smoke the opium of his brewing.

"It is a joy to have found a fellow-spirit," I sighed. "When one has opium one wants nothing more."

"How many pipes do you smoke a day?" he asked.

"Fifty," I said boldly, adding, "when I am in practice."

"That is nothing," said the Cypriote. "I smoke a hundred. Come, let us begin. Time is empty, except for opium."

"But who will prepare our pipes?" I asked.

"We will do that ourselves," he answered.

"I can't," I had to admit. "I—I am used to an attendant, who hands me my pipes already cooked."

"There is no one here," he said, "except an ugly old woman. But I will show you myself. Half the pleasure is lost if another hand prepares the precious fluid. See, you take a drop of opium—so—on the point of the needle, and holding it over the flame of the lamp, you turn and turn it gently until it swells and expands and glows with its hidden life. From a black drop it changes to a glowing bubble of crimson. Then you cool it again, moulding and pressing it back to a little pellet upon the glass of the lampshade. Then again you cook it, and again you cool it. Only experience can tell when it is ready to smoke. It is an art, like other arts. I would rather cook opium than write a poem. It is even better than money. Now you take your pipe and, heating the little hole through which the opium is smoked, so that it will stick, you thrust your needle—so—into the hole, and then withdraw it again, leaving the pellet of perfect peace behind. And now, lying on your left side, with your head well back amongst the cushions, you hold your pipe over the flame and draw in a long and grateful breath. In and in you breathe... ."

I watched him take a deep draught of the drug, and then lie back among the cushions with heavy-lidded eyes. For a full half-minute he remained silent and dreaming, then expelled the thick white smoke with a sigh of bliss.

It was my turn now, and not without some dismay (although curiosity was probably a stronger emotion) I accepted a pipe of his preparing. I inhaled in and in—I choked a little—and then lay back with a dreaminess that was not simulated, for it had made me feel giddy.

"You prepare a most perfect pipe," I coughed through the acrid fumes.

But I had realised immediately that I had not an opium temperament. In all I smoked ten small pipes that first evening, without feeling any ill effects beyond a heavy lassitude, which lasted all through the following day. I was disappointed and disgusted by the experience. The beautiful dreams are a myth. So also is the deadly fascination of the drug. I loathed it more each time I tasted it.

Yet those nights I lay on a sofa, *couché à gauche* as opium-smokers say, weaving a tissue of deceit into the grey-white clouds encircling us, will always remain one of the most curious memories of my life. The couches, the needles and the pipes, the pin-point pupils and wicked profile of my host, as he leaned over the green glimmer of the lamp which burnt to the god to whom his heart was given, and the growth of that god in him, as pipe followed pipe to stir his consciousness, and the beatitude that lit his features, as he looked up from amidst the cushions to that dream-world of subtle smoke, to be seen only with narrowed eyes, where princes of the poppies reign: this had a glamour against the drab setting of captivity which I will neither deny nor excuse. I was doing something practical once more. Instead of reading philosophy or playing chess, I was engaged in a human game, whose stake was freedom.

A measure of success attended my efforts, for I learnt from the Cypriote, in the course of subsequent visits to his house, that if I wished for a holiday to Constantinople it would not be difficult to arrange.

I think we were both playing a double game.

We both tried to make the other talk, he with the idea of getting information about the camp and I in the hope of picking up some hint as to where to hide in Constantinople. But card-sharpers might as well have tried to fleece each other by the three card trick. His knowledge of Constantinople seemed to be *nil*, while the information he got out of me would not have filled his opium pipe. After these excursions I used sometimes to wonder whether I was not wasting my time and health. But time is cheap in captivity, and as to health, I used to counteract the opium by counter-orgies of exercises. In the early mornings I skipped and bathed in secret, but in the daytime I tottered wanly about the streets, and whenever I saw the Cypriote I told him that I craved for *confiture*: this being our name for opium.

In my condition it was an easy matter to be sent to the doctor. I told him various astonishing stories about my health, chiefly culled from a French medical work which I found in the waiting-room of his house. Within a month I was transferred to Haidar Pasha Hospital, near Constantinople. Had I been in brutal health, the operation to my nose which was the ostensible reason of my departure would not have been considered necessary. But I had been removed from the category of suspects, and was now considered an amiable invalid.

The guard on my northward journey was more like a sick attendant than a sentry. I showed him some opium pills, which I declared were delicious to take. He evinced the greatest interest, and I was able to prevail on him to swallow two or three as an experiment. Unfortunately, after he had taken them, I discovered they contained nothing more exciting than cascara. They did not send him to sleep at all.

We arrived at Haidar Pasha without incident. Before being admitted, my effects were searched, and stored away, but being by that time accustomed to searches, I was able to hide, upon my person, a variety of things that would be useful in an escape, notably a compass, and a complete set of maps of Constantinople and its surroundings.

Captain Sir Robert Paul, with whom I had discussed plans at Afion-kara-hissar, was already installed in hospital, where he was being treated for an aural complaint. His friendship was an inestimable stand-by through the months that followed. Through scenes of farce and tragedy he was always the same feckless and fearless spirit. In success, as in adversity, he kept an equal mien. Without him, the most amusing chapters in my life would not have happened, and if I write "*I*" in the pages which follow, it is only because Robin, as I shall hereafter call him, has not been consulted about this record of our days together. Owing to circumstances beyond our control, the full responsibility for this story must be mine. The seas divide us. I cannot ask his help, or solicit his approval.

The hospital at Haidar Pasha was the most delightfully casual place imaginable. One wandered into one's ward in a Turkish nightshirt, and wandered out again at will, the only limits to peregrination being the boundaries of the hospital and one's own rather fantastic dress. Unless one asked loudly and insistently for medicines or attendance, no one dreamed of doing anything at all in the way of treatment. The only attention the patients received was to be turned out of the hospital when they were either dead or restored to health. Under the latter category a crowd of invalids came every day, who were generally ejected just before noon, clamouring loudly for their mid-day meal, and the unexpended portion of their day's ration. Of deaths in hospital I witnessed only one, although scores occurred during my stay. One evening an Armenian officer was brought into my ward with severe wounds in the head, due to a prematurely exploded bomb. He was laid flat on a bed, and instantly proceeded to choke. No one came near him. It seemed obvious to me that if he was propped up by pillows he would be able to breathe. But no one propped him up. I suggested to the hospital orderly that this should be done, and he said, "Yarin." And "yarin" the poor officer died of lack of breath. How sick men survived is a mystery to me, because they were never attended to, unless strong enough to scream. Screaming, however, is a habit to which the Turkish patient is not averse. He does not believe in the stoical repression of feeling. Strong and brave men will bellow like bulls while their wounds are being dressed. Unless, indeed, one makes a fuss, no one will believe one is being hurt. I have seen mutton-fisted dressers tearing off bandages by main force, while some unfortunate patient with a stoical tradition sweats with agony and bites his lips in silence.

But although the Turk cries out, he is by no means a coward under the knife. His stern and simple faith seems to help him here. There is something very fine about a good Moslem's readiness for death. No man who knows the religion, or has lived intimately among its adherents, can fail to give it reverence. Before God all men are equal, and when one walks about in a nightshirt, one begins to realise this fundamental truth. There was a great friendliness in that hospital, and a cordiality that coloured the otherwise sordid surroundings. Poor jettison of the war, broken with fighting, or rotten with disease, or shamming sick, we forgathered in the corridors, or in the garden, with no thought for the external advantages of rank and fortune.

Matches at that time had practically disappeared from Turkey, and whenever one issued from the ward with a cigarette between one's lips, one was beset by invalids in search of a light. Who lit the original vestal fire I do not know, but I am sure it was never extinguished in that hospital. Patients smoked and talked all night.

We took our part with pleasure in this picnic life. Robin, with remarkable skill, had contrived to smuggle in various forbidden bottles, which contributed greatly to our popularity. One drink especially, from its innocuous appearance and stimulating properties, found great favour amongst the patients. It was known as "Iran," and consisted of equal parts of sour milk and brandy. A teetotaller might safely be seen with a long glass of creamy-looking fluid, yet Omar Khayyám himself would not have despised a jug of it. Imbibing this, we used to hold polyglot pow-wows with the patients, in French, German, Arabic, Italian, and Turkish. Sugar and tea from our parcels also did much to promote cordiality.

The recent explosion in Haidar Pasha station, which blew out all the windows of our (adjacent) hospital, and the first British air raid of 1918 were frequent topics of discussion. With regard to these events we invented a beautiful lie, namely, that the station explosions were the result of bombardment by a new type of submarine we possessed, but that, *per contra*, the first air raid, which did no damage, was not carried out by British aircraft at all. We proved by assorted arguments in various languages that the bombs on Constantinople had come from German aeroplanes, the raid being a display of Hun frightfulness, to show what would happen if Turkish allegiance wavered over the thorny question of the disposal of the Black Sea fleet. Nothing was too improbable to be true in Constantinople, and nothing indeed was too absurd to be possible. Enver Pasha had made a monopoly in milk, and a corner in velvet. The new Sultan was intriguing for the downfall of the Young Turks. The funds of the Committee of Union and Progress had been sent to Switzerland, where a Turkish pound purchased thirteen francs of Swiss security, or half its face value. Fortunes were won and lost on the meteoric fluctuations of paper money. A lunatic inmate of the hospital (formerly a Smyrniote financier, driven to despair by the press gang) told me that he could make a million on the bourse if they only set him free for a few hours, and I daresay he was right. Anything might have happened during those summer days. Secret presses were engaged in printing broadsheets of revolution. The nearer the Germans got to Paris, the more persistent were the stories of their defeat. The air was electric with rumours. The story about German aeroplanes bombing Constantinople, which we had started in jest, was retailed to us later, in all earnestness, and with every detail to give it probability. Anything to the discredit of their ally found currency in the Turkish capital.

An Ottoman cadet in my ward, for instance, used to impersonate a German officer ordering his dinner in a Turkish restaurant. He managed somehow to convey the swagger, and the stays, and the stiff neck. Clattering his sword behind him, he used to seat himself stiffly at a table and call haughtily for a waiter. Then, after glaring at the menu, he used to order—a dish of haricot beans. "Des haricots," he used to snap, with hand on sword-hilt in the exact and invariable Prussian manner.

But to the last, the Germans were all-unconscious of what went on behind their corseted backs. Only at the time of the armistice, when they were pelted with rotten vegetables, did they realise that something was amiss.

To return to our hospital. Our day began with rice and broth at six in the morning. At nine the visiting doctor made his rounds and the patients who needed medicines clamoured for them. Unless one made a fuss, however, one was left in perfect peace. At midday there was more rice and broth, with occasional lumps of meat. The afternoon was devoted to sleep, and the evenings to exercise in the garden, or intrigue. Rice and broth concluded the day. This sounds dull, but after two years of prison life, the hours seemed as crowded as a London season's. To begin with, we did not attempt to subsist on hospital fare, but commissioned various orderlies and friends to buy us food outside. Then there was the never-failing interest of making plans. A certain person raised our hopes to the zenith by telling us of the possibility of a boat calling for us at night, at a landing place just below the British cemetery. The idea was to embark in this boat, row across to a steamer, and there enter large sealed boxes in which we would pass the Customs up the Bosphorus, and then make Odessa. The plan was almost complete. The shipping people had been "squared." It only remained for us to select the spot from which to embark. With this object in view, we reconnoitred the British cemetery which abutted on the hospital grounds. It was then being used as an anti-aircraft station, and when, a few days later, the first air raid came, we saw the exact positions of the Turkish machine guns, spitting lead at our aircraft from among the Crimean graves. This air raid, and the atmosphere of "frightfulness" caused thereby, rather interfered with our escape plans. First of all we were forbidden to go near the British cemetery, and later other small privileges were curtailed which greatly "cramped our style." For some time we could not get in touch with the person already alluded to.

Meanwhile the arrival of our aeroplanes was a very stimulating sight. Everyone in hospital turned out to see the show.

Crump! crump! Woof!—said the bombs.

Woo-woo-woom!—answered the Archies.

Kk-kk-kk-kk! chattered the machine guns.

"God is great," muttered the hospital staff.

"Give me a gun!" cried one of the two British officers posing as lunatics (I have already related how they had pretended to hang themselves). "Give me a gun," he reiterated loudly—"this is all a plot to kill me, and I must defend myself!"

Calmly and confidently our machines sailed through the barrage, dropped their bombs, turned to have a look at Constantinople, and then sailed away.

The British lunatic shook his fist at them, as he was led back gibbering to his ward. The head doctor was much concerned as to his condition.

"Every day," he told me—"some new madness takes that poor deluded creature. Eighteen pounds were paid to him recently and he promptly tore the notes in half and scattered them about the room. When he was asked if he wanted anything from the Embassy he wrote for a ton of carbolic soap, and half a ton of chocolate. On another occasion he jumped into the hospital pond with his pipe in his mouth, declaring he was on fire. I dare not send him to England without an escort, for he would do himself some injury. As to the other British lunatic, he has not spoken for five weeks. I do not know what is to be done."

Neither did I, for I was not then aware of the patient's true condition, and had no desire to "butt in." They had lived for several months among the other madmen in hospital, and I thought it probable that they had really lost their reason.

The lunatics' ward was a terrifying place. My experience of it, although limited to a few hours, was enough to last a lifetime. In order to secure drugs for "doping" sentries I complained of severe insomnia one day, and was sent to the mental specialist. While waiting for him, I noticed that one of the British lunatics was regarding me with unblinking furious eyes, while the other was praying—apparently for the souls of the damned. The Greek financier was singing softly to himself, and applauding himself. There is something very alarming about madness. One feels suddenly and closely what a narrow margin divides us from a world of terror. Their souls stand forlornly by their bodies, knocking at the door of intelligence.

When the mental specialist arrived, I was seized by grave alarm. What if he should find me insane? ...

He held up a finger, tracing patterns in the air, and told me to watch it closely. While I watched him, he watched me.

"The moving finger writes," I thought, "and having writ ..."

"I can see your finger perfectly," I protested nervously.

"Far from it," said the enthusiastic specialist. "You are not following it with your eyes."

"I am—indeed I am," said I, squinting at his fat forefinger.

"I am told you cannot sleep," continued my interlocutor. "You seem to me to be suffering from nervous exhaustion."

"A little sleeping draught ..." I suggested.

"I ought to observe you for a few days," he answered.

"Not here?" I quavered.

"Yes, here."

"But I do not like the—other lunatics," said I, in a small voice.

Eventually, to my great delight, I was allowed to remain where I was, and was given (as reward for the danger I had endured) several cachets of bromide and a few tablets of trional.

I returned in triumph to my ward, and Robin and I laid our heads together. With the drugs we now possessed it would be possible to send our sentries to sleep when we were moved from hospital, if the person who was making plans for us to be taken on board a Black Sea steamer failed to communicate in time. But the question now arose as to how much of these drugs was suitable for the Turkish constitution. The object was to administer a sleeping draught, not a fatal dose. If we were transferred from Haidar Pasha we knew we should be sent for a time to the garrison camp of Psamattia (a suburb of Constantinople on the European side) and our intention was to inveigle our attendants into having lunch during our journey there, and ply them with Pilsener beer, suitably prepared, until they were somnolent and unsuspicious enough to make it feasible to bolt.

Neither the bromide nor the trional could be tasted in cocoa or coffee, we discovered, so one evening, I regret to say, I carried out an experiment on a wounded patient, who was otherwise quite fit, although rather sleepless, by giving him a cachet of bromide and a tablet of trional in a cup of cocoa. In about half an hour his eyelids began to flicker, and he was soon sleeping like a lamb. Next morning he complained of a slight headache. Should he chance to read these lines I hope he will accept my apologies. *À la guerre comme à la guerre.*

So now we had the beginning of a second plan, in case the box business *via* the Black Sea failed. But, in the event of escaping during our journey to Psamattia, we had no very clear idea of where to hide. That there were Greek and Jewish quarters in Galata and in Pera we knew, and also in the northern part of Stamboul, but the chances of detection in any of these localities were great, especially as we had no disguises at the time. There remained a possibility of hiding in the ruins of recent fires, but it was difficult to see how we were to live there. On the whole the Black Sea trip seemed to offer the most favourable opportunities of success. But to carry it out, we had to wait, and wait, and still to wait, until we heard from our agent again. And eventually the time came when we could wait no longer.... .

A week or two is nothing in Turkey, but unfortunately we had attracted a certain amount of undesirable attention in hospital by our popular supper-parties and reputed wealth. There was also a Bulgarian nurse who had an uncanny intuition about our intentions. She told the visiting doctor that two other nurses were in the habit of bringing us brandy. She also said we were both quite well and had never in fact been ill at all. The latter statement was true, but the former I can only attribute to pique, the brandy having come from other sources. However, this did not affect the fact that we were politely but firmly told that we had greatly benefited by our stay in hospital. This was equivalent to a notice of dismissal. We would have to go. Thereupon we both instantly pulled very long faces, and went to see the ear and nose specialist. He was our one hope of being allowed to stay on.

While waiting for an interview, I had an opportunity of seeing an eminent army surgeon at work on the Turkish soldiers. Let me preface this description by emphasising the fact that he *was* eminent. He was no rough bungler, but a clever practitioner, well known for his professional and human sympathy. This is the scene I saw.

The doctor sat on a high stool, by the window, with a round reflector over his right eye. A glass table beside him was strewn with instruments. A lower stool seated his victims. In his hand he held a thing like a small glove-stretcher. Behind him two young assistants stood, looking like choir boys who had been fighting, in their robes of blood-stained white. The room was full of miserable shivering soldiers.

A deaf old man takes the vacant seat in front of the doctor. The glove-stretcher darts into his ear. A question is asked. The old man gibbers in reply. Glove-stretcher darts into the other ear. Another question. More gibbering. Both his ears are soundly boxed, and he is sent away. The next is a goitre case, too unpleasant for description. Suddenly the attendants come forward, and pull off all his clothes. The doctor removes the reflector from his right eye, and stares for a moment at the ghastly skinny shape with a sack hanging from its throat. Then he dictates a prescription to one of the attendants, and seizes the next soldier. Prescription and clothes are thrown at the naked man, who walks out shivering, holding his apparel in his arms. Meanwhile another victim is already trembling on the stool. This man trembles so violently that he falls down in a faint. The attendants cuff him back to consciousness. Painfully he gets up and tries to face the instrument again. But as the glove-stretcher is being inserted into his nostril, he turns the colour of weak tea and again silently collapses. The doctor does not give him a second look. One of the attendants drags his limp body to a corner, while another patient takes the seat in front of the doctor. After a few more cases have been examined, the two attendants return to the unconscious man in the corner, drag him back to the doctor and hold his lolling head to the light, while the glove-stretcher does its work. Then he is pulled away, like a dummy from an arena, to the door of the consulting room, where (and here I confess I expected a scene) a woman awaited him. But she seemed to consider it all in the day's work. Perhaps poor Willie was subject to fainting fits... .

I knew I would not faint, but I cannot say I took my turn on that seat with a light heart. The surgeon was alarmingly sudden, and already the room looked like a shambles.

To my relief, he used a new glove-stretcher.

"Slightly deflected septum," he pronounced, and his diagnosis was later confirmed in London.

"I hurt my nose boxing," I explained conversationally, "and cannot now breathe through it. I would like to stay——"

"Can't stay here." he said instantly and incisively; "no time to deal with your case."

"But I can't breathe through my nose."

"Breathe through your mouth," he suggested kindly, but a little coldly.

Now, it is impossible to "wangle" a man who sits over you with a reflecting mirror screwed into his right eye. I vanished with suitable thanks.

Robin had better luck with his ear. He could have stayed on in hospital and would very likely have been invalided back to England eventually. But he absolutely refused to exchange the comfortable security of a bodily affliction for the vivider joys of escape. In spite of my advice to stay in hospital, he decided, to my great delight, that we would try our luck together.

All hope of remaining in hospital was now at an end.

That evening at sunset we were in the garden, looking across the blue waters of the Marmora to the mosques and minarets of old Stamboul, flushed with the loveliest tints of pink.

It was the last evening but one of Ramazan. To-morrow the crescent of the new moon would appear over the dome of San Sofia, as a sign to all that the fast had ended, and the time of rejoicing come. Between that moon and the next moon an unknown future lay before us. And whatever our fate, it was sure to be something exciting.

CHAPTER VIII

OUR FIRST ESCAPE

Our crossing from Haidar Pasha to the garrison camp at Psamattia was a tame affair. Early in the day we had made up our minds that it would be unwise to escape, as well as unkind to our indulgent sentries: unwise, because we realised that if we bolted blindly from a restaurant, we would probably be caught at the first lodging-house at which we tried to gain admission; and unkind because, in common chivalry, we decided that our sentries were too trustful to be drugged.

Our day, therefore, was spent in seeing the sights of Pera, gossiping over a cocktail bar, purchasing some illicit maps under cover of a large quantity of German publications, and generally learning the lie of the land. But it might be indiscreet even at this distance of time to describe in too great detail the sources from which we obtained our information. One name, however—like King Charles' head with Mr. Dick—will keep coming into this book. I cannot keep it out, because it is impossible to think of my escape and escapades without thinking of the gallant lady who made them possible.

Miss Whitaker, as she then was (she is now Lady Paul), knew something about all the escapes which took place in Turkey, and a great deal about a great many of them. Against every kind of difficulty from foes, and constant discouragement from friends[6] she boldly championed the cause of our prisoners through the dark days of 1916 and 1917. She visited the sick in hospital, she carried plum puddings to our men working at San Stefano, she was a never-failing source of sympathy and encouragement. She sent messages for us, and wrote letters, and lent us money and clothes. She was the good angel of the English at Constantinople, a second—and more fortunate— Miss Cavell.

And she was the *Deus ex machina* of my escapes. Having said this, I will say one thing more. I cannot here put down one-tenth of the daring work that Lady Paul did for me and others. The reason may be obvious to the reader; at any rate it is binding on me to say far less than I would wish.

On reaching the prisoners' camp at Psamattia, our first object was to get in touch with her whom we had already heard of as the guardian spirit of prisoners. With this object in view, we asked to be allowed to attend Sunday service at the English church. Religious worship, we pointed out, should not be interfered with, further than the necessities of war demanded. After some demur the Commandant agreed, and accordingly we went to church. Here it was[7] that we met our guardian angel for the first time. She trembled visibly when we mentioned our plans for escape, and I thought (little knowing her) that we had been rash to speak so frankly.

"I strongly advise delay," she whispered—"but I will meet you again at the gardens in Stamboul in two days' time—four o'clock. I'll be reading a———"

"*Haidé, effendim, haidé, haidé*," said our sentry, and her last words were lost.

Further conversation was impossible, but the forty-eight hours which followed were vivid with anticipation.

How were we to manage to get to the gardens of the Seraglio? Would we meet her? Could we talk to her? Would she have a plan? ...

On the day appointed, Robin and I complained of toothache, and asked to be allowed to go into the city to see the dentist. We were at once granted permission.

From the dentist's to the Seraglio garden was only a step, but we were four hours too early as yet to keep the rendezvous. However, a large lunch, in which our sentries shared, smoothed the way for a little shopping excursion into Pera. Here, amongst other things, we bought some black hair dye, which completed our arrangements for escape. Other paraphernalia, such as jack-knives, twenty fathoms of rope, maps, compasses, sand-shoes, chocolate and "dope," we had already acquired. Nothing now remained but to find a hiding place, when once we had escaped.

At about three o'clock we were sitting in a café, eating ices, with our complacent sentries, who had every reason to be complacent for they had been sumptuously fed, as well as liberally tipped. They were quite willing to do anything in reason, and nothing could have been more natural than a stroll in the Seraglio gardens.

But just then Robin began to get "Spanish 'flu," which was raging in the city. The symptoms were as sudden as they were unmistakable. Violent shivering, giddiness, weakness—all the ills that flesh is heir to, waylaid him at this vital juncture. He was completely incapable of action.

There was no help for it. I left him shaking and shivering in the café, in charge of one of our two sentries, and, after a little persuasion and some palaver (during the course of which another bank-note changed hands) I induced the other sentry to accompany me for a stroll. Unless we walked in the gardens, I assured him, we should both fall ill with the deadly contagion of my friend. Nothing but fresh air and iced beer could avert that fever. On the way, therefore, we stopped for a glass and I managed to drop a small dose of potassium bromide into the sentry's mug before it was given to him.

A little before four the sentry and I were smoking cigarettes on a seat in the Seraglio gardens quite close to the Stamboul entrance gate.

It was a hot day, with thunder-clouds hanging low. Toilers of the city passed us fanning themselves. Turkish officers had pushed back their heavy fur fezzes, and civilians wore handkerchiefs behind theirs. German ladies panted loudly, and even the *hanoums* appeared to be a little jaded: their small feet and great eyes, that so often twinkle in the streets, had grown dull with the oppression of the day. Small wonder my sentry nodded.

Presently, with a walk that no one could mistake, a tall and slim figure entered, dressed in white serge coat and skirt. I watched her, on the opposite footpath, strolling down the shady avenue with an insouciant grace. She held a novel and a little tasselled bag in her right hand. She sat down some two hundred yards away, and began reading calmly and coolly, apparently quite unconscious of the feverish world about her.

With a hasty glance at my sentry, I rose and walked very slowly away. He woke at once, and followed. I stopped to look at some flowers, yawned, lit another cigarette and said to the sentry that it was too hot to walk. I intended to sit for a little in the shade on the opposite side of the road, and then we would go back to join our friend at the café.

We meandered across the road, and I sank into a seat beside the guardian angel. There was no room for the sentry, so he obligingly retired into the shrubbery behind.

Without taking her eyes from her novel, she began by saying I was not to look at her, and that I was to speak very low, looking in the opposite direction.

She then asked where my companion was, and on hearing he had the 'flu, she told me that she also had been attacked by it at the very moment that we had spoken to her at church, and that it was only with difficulty she had been able to keep the rendezvous to-day. I tried to thank her for coming, but she kept strictly to business, and concentrated our conversation to bare facts. Her news ranged from the world at war, to plans for Robin and me, in vivid glimpses of possibility. She covered continents in a phrase, and dealt with the plans of two captives in terse but sympathetic comment. When she had told me what she wanted to say, she opened her small bag and took out a piece of paper, rolled up tight, which she flicked across to me without a moment's hesitation.

"You had better go now," she said.

But my heart was brimming over with things unsaid.

"I simply cannot thank——" I began to stammer.

"Don't!" said she, to the novel on her knees.

And so, with no salute to mark the great occasion, I left her. Neither of us had seen the other's face.

Here I must apologise for purposely clouding the narrative. The plans I made are only public so far as they concern myself.

On rejoining Robin, I found him palpitant and perturbed. The fever was at its height and he ought to have been in bed. Yet it was urgently necessary that evening, before returning, to make certain investigations in the native quarter of the city. How to do this without attracting the notice of the two sentries, perspiring but still perceptive, was a matter of great concern to me. I thought of saying that I was going to buy medicine for Robin, but in that case one of the sentries (probably Robin's, for my own had grown very somnolent with beer and bromide) would certainly accompany me. Then I bethought me of going to wash my hands in a place behind the café and slipping out of a back door. But there was no back door, and Robin's sentry had followed me to the wash-place, and stood stolidly by the door until I came out.

I sat down again, thinking and perspiring furiously,[8] and ordered more beer. But this time I failed to manipulate the bromide. Robin's sentry saw me with the packet in my hand and asked me what it was.

"It is a medicine for reducing fat," said I, and of course after this I had to keep the drugged beer for myself. But the sedative did no harm. After sipping for some minutes I had a happy thought.

There was a particular brand of cigarettes which were only obtainable at a few shops in Constantinople. I asked the waiter if he had them. He had not.

"I must have a packet," I said, standing up—"there is a shop just down the street where I can get them."

And without taking my hat or stick (as a proof of the innocence of my intentions) I strolled out of the café.

The sentries did not follow. It was too hot.

I rushed down the crowded thoroughfare as if all the hounds of heaven were on my trail. I fled past policemen, dodged a tram, bolted up a side-street, and arrived gasping at the doorway I sought. After a hasty survey of the locality, so as to identify it again at need, I rushed back to the restaurant, buying a box of Bafra-Madène cigarettes on the way. Robin was still shivering; the sentries were mopping their large faces. All was well. Our work was done.

Trying not to look triumphant, I got Robin into a cab, and we drove back to Psamattia camp.

During the next few days I thoroughly enjoyed myself. Not so Robin, who was grappling with his fever. Later, however, when he was convalescent, we used to go down to the seashore together to bathe. In the evening, we used to sup off lobsters at a restaurant on the beach. In the water one felt almost free once more, and in the restaurant, when one was not gambling "double or quits" with the lobster-merchant as to whether we should pay him two pounds for his lobster or nothing at all, we were talking politics with other diners. Those days of Robin's convalescence were delightful. The moon was near its full, which is the season when lobsters ought to be eaten, and the climate was perfect, and our hopes were high.

Psamattia is one of the most westerly suburbs of Stamboul. From it, a maze of tortuous streets lead to the railway terminus of Sirkedji, and the Galata bridge over the Golden Horn. On the eastern side of the Golden Horn lie the European quarters of Galata and Pera. From our camp at Psamattia to the house where we intended to hide was a distance of five miles, and there were at least two police posts on the way. But with our hair dyed black (we had already effected this transformation, and it is astonishing how it changes one's appearance) and fezzes on our heads, we trusted to pass unnoticed as Greeks.

Our plan had a definite and limited objective. We wanted to escape by night from Psamattia and hide in Constantinople. Once in hiding, we trusted to going by boat to Russia, or else going with brigands to the Mediterranean coast, where our patrols might pick us up. But the first object was to get away from the camp. Until this was achieved it was almost impossible to make definite arrangements. At first we had thought that it would be an easy matter to give our sentries the slip when we were out shopping. But when it came to the point, we felt scruples about bolting from men we had bribed and wheedled so often. All's fair in love and war, but yet if it could be avoided we did not want to abuse their trust in us.

There remained the alternative of escaping by night from the house where we were interned. But when Robin had become fit enough to try (and of course he was all agog to be off at the first possible moment) we found the guards were more alert than we thought.

Our situation was roughly this: We were housed in the Armenian Patriarchate, next to the Psamattia Fire Brigade, and there were sentries in every street to

which access was possible, by craft or by climbing. The window of our room, which was directly over the doorway where the main guard lived, looked out on to a narrow street, across which there was another house, inhabited by Russian prisoners of war. At first we thought it might be possible to pretend to go to the Russian house, and, while casually crossing the street, to mingle with the passers-by, and melt away unnoticed in the crowd. We tried this plan, but it was no good. The guards on our doorway were alert, and followed our every movement.... To slip out with the Armenian funerals which used to go through our gateway was another project doomed to failure.... To get into the Armenian church, on the night before a burial, remove the occupant of a coffin and so pass out next morning in the centre of the funeral procession, was an idea which excited us for a time. But the melodrama we had planned could not be executed, because the church was locked and guarded at night...
. To climb out of the back window of the Russian house also proved impossible, because a sentry stood outside it always.... Every point was watched. Two sentries armed with old Martini rifles (of archaic pattern but unpleasantly big bore) were posted directly below our window. Two more similarly equipped were opposite, at the door of the Russian house. One man with a new rifle was behind the Russian house. Two more were behind ours, and one was in a side street. There were also men on duty at the entrance to the Fire Brigade.

After considering all sorts of methods we decided on a plan whose chief merit was its seeming impossibility. No one would have expected us to try it.

Our idea was to climb out of our window at night, and by crossing some ten foot of wall-face, to gain the shelter of the roof of the next door house. This roof was railed by a parapet, behind which we could crouch. Along it we would creep, until we reached a cross-road down the street. Here we would slip down a rope to the pavement, and although we would be visible to at least five sentries during our descent, it seemed probable that no particular sentry would consider himself responsible for the cross-roads, which was beyond their beat.

To climb out of a window set in a blank wall, about thirty feet above a busy street where four sentries stood, did not seem a reasonable thing to do. But the wall was not as impassable as it seemed. Two little ledges of moulding ran along it, under our window-sill, so that we had a narrow yet sufficient foothold and handhold until we reached the roof of the adjoining house. And although we would be visible during our precarious transit of the wall-face, we knew that people rarely look up above their own height, and rarely look for things they don't expect.

It was the night of the twenty-seventh of July, when a bright full moon rode over the sea behind our house, that we decided to make the attempt.

The first point was to get out of the window without being seen.... A Colonel of the Russian Guards, a little man with a great heart, volunteered to help us. Directly we extinguished the lights in our room, he was to engage the sentries at the door of the opposite house, where he lived, in an animated conversation, keeping them interested, even by desperate measures if need be, until our first ten yards of climbing was successfully accomplished.

After a cordial good-bye, he left us. We took off our boots and slung them round our necks, drank a stirrup cup to our success, roped ourselves together, coiled the remainder of the rope round our waists, stuffed our pockets and knapsacks with our escaping gear, and then blew out our lamp, as if we were going to bed. Crouched under the window-sill we waited.... The sentries below us were sitting on stools in the street. The two men opposite were lolling against the doorpost, and the moon, rising behind our house, while still leaving the street in shadow, had just caught their faces, so that their every eyelash was visible. To them came the little Colonel, and only the top of his cap reached the moonlight. We heard his cheery voice. We saw both sentries looking down, presumably helping themselves to his cigarettes.

That waiting moment was very tense. An initial failure would have been deplorable, yet many things made failure likely. At such times as these, the confidence of one's companion counts for much, and I shall never forget Robin's bearing. Anyone who has been in similar circumstances will know what I mean. He went first out of the window. I followed an instant later.... And once the first step was taken, once my feet were on that two-inch ledge and my hands clung to the upper strip, the complexion of things altered completely. Anxiety vanished, leaving nothing but a thrill of pleasure. One was master of one's fate.

At one moment we were in view of four sentries (two at our door and two opposite), a Turkish officer who had come to take the air at our doorway, and several passers-by in the street. But no one looked up. No one saw the two men, only five yards away, who clambered slowly along the string-course, like flies on a wall.

After gaining the roof of the next house, we lay flat and breathless behind the parapet, and thanked God we had succeeded in—not making fools of ourselves, anyway.

The parapet was lower than we thought, and in order to get the advantage of its cover it was necessary to remain absolutely prone in the gutter of the roof. In this position, from ten o'clock till half past eleven, we wriggled and wriggled along the house-tops, past a dead cat and other offensive objects, until at last we had covered the distance. Once, during this stalk, my rope got hitched up on a nail, and I had to wriggle back to free it. And once, having raised myself to take a look round, one of the sentries on the Russian house ran out into the street and started making a tremendous noise. I don't know what it was about, but it alarmed me very much, and condemned us to marble immobility for a time.

At last, however, we reached the end of our wriggle. But here a new difficulty confronted us. Directly overlooking the part of the roof from which we contemplated our descent, and less than ten yards away, an officer of the Psamattia Fire Brigade sat at an open window, looking anxiously up and down the street, as if expecting someone to keep an appointment. His window was on a level with us. So intently did he stare that I thought he had seen us. But we lay dead-still behind the parapet, and it became apparent, as time passed and he still stood disconsolate by the window, that we were not the objects of his languishing regard... . And meanwhile the moon—the kindly old moon that sees so much—was creeping up the sky. Soon she would flood us with her radiance. Even a love-sick officer of the Fire Brigade could not fail to notice us across the narrow street, lit by the limelight of all the universe. For an hour this annoying Romeo kept watch, while we discussed the situation in tiny whispers, and cursed feminine unpunctuality. But at last, just as we had determined to "let go the painter" and take our chance, he began to yawn and stretch and look towards his bed, which we could see at the further end of his room. "You are tired of waiting: she isn't worth it!" I sent in thought-wave across the street. He seemed to hesitate, then he yawned again, and just as our protecting belt of shadow had narrowed to a yard, he gave up his hopes of Juliet, and retired.

That was our moment.

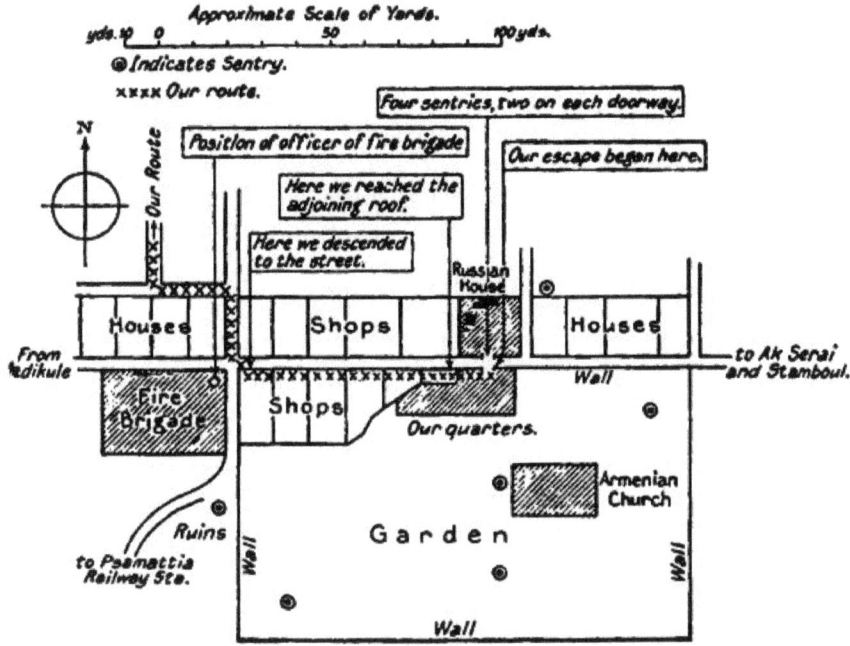

THE ARMENIAN PATRIARCHATE AT PSAMATTIA, CONSTANTINOPLE.

We stood up, and made the rope fast to a convenient ring in the parapet. Traffic in the street had ceased. The sentries were huddled in their coats, for it was a chilly summer night. Up street, a dog was yapping, and its voice seemed to stab the silence. Before stepping over the parapet I took a last look at the world I left and thanked God.

The waiting was over. In two seconds' time we should have gained freedom, or a slug from some sentry's rifle.

It took two seconds to slip down thirty feet of rope, and two seconds is a long time when your liberty, if not your life, is at stake. I half kicked down the signboard of a shop in my descent, and Robin, who followed, completed the disaster. In our haste, we had cut our hands almost to the bone, and had made noise enough to wake the dead.

Yet no one stirred. We were both in the street, and no one had moved.

After two and a half years of captivity we were free men once more. The slothful years had vanished in the twinkling of an eye. Can you realise the miracle, liberty-loving reader, that passes in the mind of a man who thus suddenly realises his freedom? ...

I don't know what Robin thought, for we said nothing. We lit cigarettes and strolled away. But inside of me, the motors of the nervous system raced.

The only other danger, in our hour and a half's walk to our destination, was being asked for passports by some policeman. In our character as polyglot mechanics, whenever we passed anyone, I found it a great relief to make some such remark as:

> Lieb Vaterland, magst ruhig sein,
> Fest steht and treu die Wacht am Rhein.

But Robin, who could not understand my German, paid little heed.

Only once we did think we were likely to be re-caught. At about one in the morning, as we were passing the Fatih mosque, we heard a rattle on the cobbles behind us. A carriage was being galloped in our direction. It might well contain some of the Psamattia garrison. We doubled into some ruins, and lay there, while the clatter grew louder and louder.

A few wisps of cloud crossed the moon, that had reached her zenith. Their silent shadows moved like ghosts across the desolation of the city. A cat was abroad. She saw us, and halted, with paw uplifted and blazing eyes.

Then the carriage passed, empty, with a drunken driver. It rattled away into the night, and we emerged, and took our way through the streets of old Stamboul, under the chequered shade of vines.

[6] This applies in no way to the Americans, who did everything possible for our men before they left Constantinople. Their assistance was always of the most prompt and practical nature. It may be invidious to mention names in this light account of adventure, but I cannot refrain from giving myself the pleasure of saying how grateful I am to Mr. Hoffman Phillips, of the American Embassy. His name, as also the name of his chief, Mr. Morgenthau, is indissolubly connected with our early prisoners. I wish to thank him from the bottom of my heart, and I know many of all ranks who will join with me in this—far too meagre—tribute to his activities and ability.

[7] Let no one think the clergyman in charge aided or abetted our secular efforts to escape. On the contrary, on a later occasion, when Robin, as a poor and distressed prisoner hiding from the Turks, endeavoured to find sanctuary for a few hours in the church, he was expelled therefrom, so that our enemies should not complain that the House of God was used for anything but worship.

[8] During the afternoon I lost over seven pounds in weight.

CHAPTER IX

A CITY OF DISGUISES

We knocked softly at the door of the house that was to be our home, and then waited, flattened in the shadow below it, quite prepared for the worst. It was then four o'clock in the morning. It seemed too much to hope that we would be welcome.

But we were. The door opened cautiously about one inch, and two little faces were seen, low down the crack. Behind them, someone held a light.

Then the door was flung wide, and we saw on the stairs a whole family of friendly people, male and female, old and young, all in night dress, and all with arms outstretched in rapturous greeting. We might have been Prodigal Sons returning, instead of two strangers whose presence would be a source of continual danger.

Hyppolité and Athéné, the twins, aged eight, who had first peeped at us, now took us each by the hand, and led us upstairs.

"The last escaped prisoner we had here was a forger," said Hyppolité to us.

"He was a friend of father's," added Athéné over her shoulder, "and he escaped from prison about six weeks ago. He was afraid that the police would find his tools, so he threw them all into our cistern. They are there now."

We reached the top floor, and were shown by the twins into an apartment containing a double bed with a stuffy canopy of damask.

"This is the family bedroom," they said.

"And where are we to sleep?" I asked.

"Here," said Thémistoclé, the proud owner of the house. "My sister and I and the twins were using the bed until your arrival, but now we will sleep in the passage."

"The passage?" I echoed. "Haven't you any other beds, and were you all four using this one?"

"Yes, yes. The other rooms are full of lodgers. There are three officers of the Turkish army here at present. But they won't disturb you, because they are hiding too."

"Mon Dieu!" said I, sitting on the bed—"but your sister can't sleep in the passage, can she?"

"Certainly, she's quite used to that sort of thing. It's safer also, in case the police come."

"I know all the police," said Athéné, "even when they are not in uniform; I can recognise them by their boots."

"And we are always on the look-out for them," added Hyppolité. "If the police come to search the house you will have to get into the cistern."

"Where the forger threw his tools," explained Athéné.

Coffee and cigarettes were produced, and ointment for our lacerated hands. We were made to feel quite at home... . The family stayed and talked to us until dawn broke. They thoroughly appreciated the story of the escape, and clapped their hands with glee at the idea of the Turks' amazement when they discovered that we had vanished, leaving no trace behind us.

"They will never find the rope," said Thémistoclé, "because the shopkeeper over whose shop it is will certainly cut it down and hide it, for fear of being asked questions."

"And now we must thank the Blessed Saints for your escape," said an old lady who had not previously spoken.

She went to a glass cupboard, opened it, and lit two candles. A scent of rose-leaves and incense came from the shrine, which contained oranges and ikons and Easter eggs and a large family Bible.

For a moment or two we all stood silent.

Then——

Just when I was expecting a prayer, the old lady blew out the candles and shut up the cupboard and crossed herself. The thanksgiving was over, and we dispersed with very cordial good-nights. I think Thémistoclé wanted to kiss us, but we felt we had been through trials enough for the time and refused to offer even one cheek.

The family retired to the passage and settled down to rest with squeaks and giggles, while Robin and I, after thanking God for all His mercies, with very humble and grateful hearts, threw ourselves down on the bed, too exhausted to undress, and slept the sleep of free men.

Next instant, it seemed to me, although in reality two hours had elapsed, we were awakened by the twins, who looked on us as their especial charges, and thought us tremendous fun.

"Time to get up," they said excitedly. "The house might be searched at any minute."

Instantly we were afoot.

"Where are the police?" I asked.

"There is a detective standing at the corner of our street," said Hyppolité.

"And they often come to see if all our lodgers are registered!" added his sister.

We bundled our maps, compasses, and other belongings into a towel, and staggered downstairs, with fear and sleep battling for mastery in our minds.

But in the pantry, we found the seniors of the household quite unconcerned. There was no imminent danger of a search.... On the other hand, there was the immediate prospect of breakfast.

A saucepan was actually being buttered (and butter was worth its weight in gold) to make us an omelette. By now we had been thoroughly stirred from sleep, and realised how hungry we were. I forget how many omelettes we ate, or how much butter we used, but I think that that charming breakfast cost a five-pound note, or thereabouts.

When it was over, an engaging sense of drowsiness began to creep over me again, but the twins were adamant.

"You must practise getting into the cistern," said Hyppolité.

"Like the forger did," chimed in Athéné—"and then you must arrange a hiding-place for your things."

The worst of it was, that their suggestions were so practical. Obviously it was our duty to at once take all precautions.

I consequently took off my clothes, and removing the lid of the cistern, I was let down through a hole in the floor into the waters below. In my descent I re-opened the wounds in my hands, and it was in no very cheerful mood that I found myself in darkness, with water up to my shoulders. I moved cautiously about, trying to imagine our feelings if fate drove us to this chilly and conventional hiding-place while detectives were conducting a search for us above. Then I barked my foot on something hard, and stooping down through the water I picked up a large block of pumicestone, which was doubtless the forger's engraving die. Something scurried on an unseen ledge; a rat no doubt. I felt I had seen enough of the cistern. Groping my way back to the lid, my fingers touched a little thing that cracked under them, and instantly I felt a stinging pain. Whether it was a beetle or a sleepy wasp I did not stop to inquire.

"Lemme get out," I bleated through the hole in the floor.... "Robin," I said, when I was safe once more, "if ever we are driven down there, we must take something to counteract the evil spirits."

All that morning we passed in the pantry, eating and dozing by snatches.

Morning merged into afternoon, the afternoon lengthened into evening, and no policeman came. We were safe.

At nightfall, after sending Hyppolité as a scout up the stairs to see that the other lodgers were not about, we ascended to our room again, and settled down definitely.

Our stay, we then thought, might last several weeks, so as to give us leisure to weigh the reliability of the various routes and guides that offered. There was no particular hurry. The longer we stayed, the more likely the Turks would be to relax such measures as they had taken for our recapture.

But we had reckoned without our host: the host of vermin. They were worse in this room than in any other place I have seen in Turkey, not excepting the lowest dungeons of the military prison, where they breed by the billion. Their voracity and vehemence made a prolonged stay impossible. Except for the first sleep of two hours, when exhaustion had made us insensible, we never thereafter had more than a single hour of uninterrupted rest.

Throughout the long and stifling nights of our stay, Robin and I lay in the stately double bed, wondering wearily how any man or woman alive could tolerate the creatures that crawled over its mahogany-posts and swarmed over its flowered damask. Every three-quarters of an hour, one or other of us used to light a candle, and add to the holocaust of creatures we had already slain.

"What hunting?" I used to ask sleepily.

"A couple of brace this time, and a cub I chopped in covert," Robin would say.

"That makes twenty-two couple up to date—and the time is 12.35 a.m."

Then at one o'clock it was Robin's turn to ask what sport I had had.

"A sounder broke away under your pillow," I reported. "Six rideable boar and six squeakers."

Ugh!

Those first days of our liberty were a trying time. To the external irritation of insects were added the mental anxieties of our situation. What, for instance, would happen to the twins if we were caught in that house? And, again, was Thémistoclé faithful? Would he be tempted by the reward offered for our recapture? At times we were not quite certain. He used to talk very gloomily about the risks and the cost of life.

"Everyone is starving," he used to say thoughtfully—"even the policemen go hungry for bribes. A friend of mine, a policeman, said to me the other day: 'For the love of Allah find somebody for me to arrest. Among all the guilty and the innocent in this town, surely you can find somebody that we could threaten to arrest? Then we would share the proceeds.'"

"What did you say to that?" I asked.

"I said," he answered thoughtfully, "that I would do my best."

"But what sort of man would you arrest?" I asked.

"Any sort of man. A drunkard perhaps, if I saw one, or a rich man, if I dared."

"Rich men are apt to be dangerous," said I meaningly.

"I know. But what can one do?" he asked, spreading out his hands. "One must live!"

"And let live," said I, thinking suddenly of the bugs, and wondering what Thémistoclé thought of them.

It was then that I noticed his method of combating the household pets.

Previously I had observed that the ends of his pyjamas (we always talked at night) were provided with strong tapes, which were tied close to his ankles; but the object of this fastening only became apparent when I noticed the excited throngs of insects on his elastic-sided boots. They could not get higher. They were balked of their blood. If he ever felt any discomfort, he merely tightened the tapes.

After a careful study of Thémistoclé's psychology (which was so full of outlooks new to me that I never achieved more than a glimpse into the pages of his past) I came to the conclusion that he was implicitly to be trusted. In his frail frame there burned a spirit of adventure and a courage that might "step from star to star." His soul had been born to live in a great man, only somehow it had made a mistake and taken a tenement instead of a manor-house to live in... .

I think sunset and sunrise were the pleasantest hours in our new abode. It was possible then to draw back the blinds without any danger of being seen, and enjoy the cool of the evening and the magnificent view which our situation afforded. Our house, although it stood in a side street, commanded a prospect of the upper end of the Golden Horn, as well as a view of one of the most populous thoroughfares of the town.

We used to sit and gaze at the twilit city, until the creeping darkness overtook us.

If circulation be a test of a city's vitality, then Constantinople was certainly at a low ebb. The pedestrians seemed to get nowhere. They were hanging about, waiting for something to happen. The whole town was dead-tired, unspeakably bored of life as it had to be lived under the Young Turks. Constantinople was getting cross... . Cross, like someone who was tired of adulation from the wrong person. Some trick of sea and sun give her this human quality of sex. Anyone who has lived for long in her houses must feel her personality. She is the courtesan of conquerors, but inherent in her is some witchcraft, by which she weakens those who hold her, so that they die and are utterly exterminated, while she remains with her fadeless and fatal beauty, an Eastern Lorelei beside the Bosphorus... . She sapped the strength of the Roman Empire, she overthrew the dominion of the Greeks, and now, after a period of fretful wedlock, she was shaking herself free from the Turk.

Something was going to happen soon. One felt it in the air.

What happened to us, was that it became necessary to draw the blinds and light our candle, and search for the pestilence that crept by night. Presently our meal arrived, which was always a cheerful interlude, but it was as short as it was sweet, for courses were few, with famine prices prevailing. Afterwards we continued our hunting till dawn.

At dawn, when the chill of morning had sent our sated enemies to sleep, there was another truce from trouble. We used to draw back the blinds again and sit at the window.

I used to watch the pale sun on the horizon, fighting the mist-forms that clung heavily to earth and sea, and I felt that in the world-consciousness a similar contest swayed. The old ideas of government were being caught by a light that was pale now, but soon to grow luminous—a radiance that would dispel the night of war, and show us a new world, intangible yet, but dimly sensed.

In the dim alleys and side streets below, where balconies overhung, shutting out the dawn, what a weight of woe there was! Famine and fire, twin angels of destruction that lurked in every by-way of the city, were waiting to take their toll. And the war went on for caged and free, while some starved and others made fortunes, and some became generals and others corpses. And the end of these things was vanity. *Vanitas vanitatum.*

The minaret of a mosque was directly opposite to me. Under sway of the sanctuary and the hour, the voice of the *muezzin* spoke to me in all its sincerity and unity of purpose. God was everywhere, all-pervasive, all-unseen, invisible only because He was so manifest. Evil of the night and glory of the dawn made His picture, the world. With new eyes I saw now this city grey with sin, and fresh with the promise of another day.

From the house of that stern and simple faith that is the creed of one-fifth of the world, there came a sense of kinship with all the suffering under the sky. Reverence came to me also, and that brotherhood which is the message of the Great Teachers since time began. These thoughts were round me, a silent company, as I looked Mecca-wards, to the place of prayer. Then the heralds of the dawn alighted on the minaret, and their wings were amethyst and saffron. The night was over, and the *muezzin's* long, exultant call to worship died down with the increasing light.

Another day had begun.

Not many days and nights did we tarry in Thémistoclé's house. Robin decided to try his luck by land. After various inquiries, he made arrangements with a Greek boy to board a melon-boat bound for Rodosto. His idea was to make that port, and thence work his way to Enos, where he hoped to be picked up by our patrol-boats. After many adventures and perils by land and sea, and a great deal of bad luck, he was caught at the town of Malgara. So ended a very gallant attempt, which ought to be set down in detail by him.

I can only describe his appearance when he left. His disguise was a matter of great difficulty, for he is so tall and so Saxon that he always attracted notice in an Eastern crowd. An Arab ragamuffin seemed the rôle best suited to him, and he accordingly exchanged his comparatively respectable clothes for a greasy old coat and a pair of repellent trousers. With a tattered fez well back on his head, and all his visible skin blackened with burnt cork, he looked an unspeakable scoundrel. But he was too villainous. He would have been immediately arrested for his appearance alone. A touch of genius, however, completed his make-up.... In his hands he carried a poor little bowl of curds and half a cucumber, which completely altered his ferocious air by adding the requisite touch of pathos. The edible emblems of innocence he carried transformed him completely into a sort of male Miss Muffet.

No detective could have found heart to inquire where he was going. He was enough to make anyone cry.

He left in a frightful hurry, for his boat was due to catch a certain tide, but we drank a stirrup cup to his success, and parted with much sadness on my side, not until the old lady before mentioned had lit a candle before the ikon of Saint Nicholas.... .

I was very sorry to see him go, but I was quite convinced (wrongly, as events proved) that the best chance of success lay in going to Russia.

The little Colonel of the Russian Guards had told us before we escaped that he was likely to be soon repatriated (for he was a person of influence in the Caucasus), and I felt sure that I could arrange to go as his servant, if no better scheme presented itself in the meanwhile. But there were many possibilities in the "city of disguises."

During my stay with Thémistoclé I had been learning history, as it is never written, but as it is most strangely lived by a people on the brink of dissolution and disaster. As an escaped prisoner I thought that delay in Constantinople—somewhere clean, however—would not be time wasted if one was in touch with the politics of the time. If the Russian scheme failed, there were other openings, by earth and air and water.

But the first thing to do was to find a place where I could lay my head without getting it bitten.

The good angel of prisoners came to my assistance at this critical juncture in my affairs.

"You must be disguised as a girl," said she—"I will buy you a wig at once."

"But what about my figure?" I asked, "and my feet ...?"

"Some clothes were left with me at the beginning of the war," she answered, "which will fit you with the help of a tailor. And as to your shoes, your own will pass muster, with new bows. No one has had any proper shoes for ages here. But you will want—well, lots of other things."

And I certainly *did* want a lot, before I looked at all presentable. After very careful shaving, I began to splash about confidently at my toilet table. There was Vesuvian black for the eyebrows, *bistre* for the eyelashes, *poudre violette*, rouge, carmine—more powder—more rouge—at last I showed my satisfied face to Miss Whitaker, who gave a cry of horror, and flatly refused to be seen in my company.

There was nothing for it but to wash my face and start again.

This time I succeeded in making myself presentable, although a blue streak of whisker seemed always slightly visible through the powder. The wig, however, helped matters greatly, and I arranged some ringlets on my shaven cheeks.

The dressing-up was quite exciting. Silk and lace and whalebone, especially a lot of lace in front, was the basis on which I built. The foundations took some time in laying, but when finished I found to my delight that the coat and skirt belonging to Miss Whitaker's friend fitted my figure perfectly.

A few details, invisible to my eyes, were quickly corrected, and I think that when I finally emerged, with large hat at a becoming angle, I did credit to my instructress.

Gloves I had always to wear, of course, and a veil was advisable, chiefly to tone down my blinding beauty to the eyes of passers-by. Do what I would, however, I could not hide a certain artificiality in my appearance, which was most unfair to Miss Whitaker, considering that I was her companion. But I behaved as well as I possibly could.

THE AUTHOR AS A GERMAN GOVERNESS

I learned how to walk in a ladylike fashion, and how to powder my nose in an engaging manner. My arms and legs had to be kept under various restraints. A mincing gait was soon acquired, but I found sitting still more awkward. My knees evinced an almost ineradicable tendency to cross themselves or sprawl, while my gloved forearms, to the last, felt as unwieldy as a baboon's. But everything I could I learned assiduously and in dead earnest, down to managing my veil, and patting my curls nicely in front of a looking-glass. It was so frightfully important not to make a false step.

My only excuse for going about with Miss Whitaker at all was the complete success of the rôle for which she had so skilfully prepared me. Never for a moment was there any suspicion of my identity.

On one occasion, in the early days of my disguise, when we were sight-seeing at Eyoub, some Turkish ladies stopped to talk to us. I remained silent, of course, but I watched them narrowly and came to the conclusion that they saw nothing amiss. My eyes, incidentally, were as well painted as theirs. Now, if two charming and worldly-wise *hanoums* cannot detect a flaw in one's form or features, it is unlikely that any mere male could be cleverer than they.

The mere males, alas! were enthralled by my appearance. Once or twice an embarrassing situation was narrowly averted. The road behind the Pera Palace Hotel is dark, and we used to ascend it in fear and trembling. But although we were followed sometimes, no one ever presumed to speak to us.

Miss Whitaker had found me by now a delightful roof, near the house in which I took my meals, and this place was free from all life smaller than a rat. Here I was able to make my plans in peace, with no fear of treachery, for, so cleverly had Miss Whitaker arranged matters, no one knew I was not a woman.

As Mademoiselle Josephine, an eccentric German governess, who suffered from consumption (and therefore spoke very low and huskily) I used to pass my nights *à belle étoile*, after well-spent days in the docks or cafés, where my plans were maturing. The stars in their courses seemed to be on my side. No longer, as when a fretful prisoner, did I think their quiet shining was a reminder of man's minuteness in the schemes of God. I felt now that man could make his destiny. And when that destiny was shaped by hands such as those that helped me, the world was a beautiful place. Good angels were here on earth, at "our own clay-shuttered doors." ...

Two little girls, to whom I used to bring chocolates, used to come up in the evening and kiss my hand, wishing me good-night. They thought I was the most amusing governess they had ever met. Their mother, a kind old lady who offered me cough mixtures, must have thought me rather odd, but then she was prepared to make allowances for foreigners, especially in war-time. To have a reason for wishing to be inconspicuous was nothing unusual in those days, whether one was German, Jew, or Greek, or male or female.

Of various opportunities that came my way, the most practical and attractive was that suggested by the Russian Colonel. His repatriation to the Caucasus was now only a matter of days. He had not only got his own passport, but also a passport for a servant. That servant was to be myself. In order to discuss plans, we found the safest rendezvous was the open-air café of the Petits Champs. This place was crowded with "fashionable" people, and although both he and Miss Whitaker were constantly shadowed by detectives there was nothing at all suspicious in their being seen at tea-time in the company of an elegantly dressed German lady.

The German lady was obviously not as young as she tried to appear, but then there was nothing unusual about that. She was also rather *gauche* in her movements, but this again was not out of keeping with the part.

"In a fortnight's time we will be having tea at Tiflis," the Russian Colonel used to say. "I will raise two regiments of cavalry and take them to kill the Bolsheviks. You shall be my adjutant."

"With the greatest pleasure in the world, *mon Colonel*. But please do not speak so loud."

"Ah, that *sacré* detective. I had forgotten him. Soon we will not have to think of such things."

"Yes, but at the present moment your own particular shadow is trying to listen to what you are saying," I remarked in low tones.

At once the Colonel's voice assumed a softer note, and his green eyes began to melt with tenderness.

"*Mais Josephine, ma petite, écoutes donc, je t'adore*... . There, he's passed. Everything is ready. I have got you a Russian soldier's uniform. You have only to put this on, and follow me on board when I go."

"And if someone asks me who I am?"

"You are my Georgian servant. And you can only speak Georgian. Just say this——"

There followed a tongue-twisting sentence, which I tried to memorise.

Meanwhile the band played, and people passed, and inquisitive eyes were turned in our direction.

"That's a spy who knows me," Miss Whitaker would say. "*Encore une tasse, mademoiselle? Non?* I think we ought to be going."

"We'll settle the final details to-morrow," I whispered.

"Right! Remember to let your beard grow. I couldn't have a smooth-faced orderly."

"*Eh bien, mille mercis, Colonel*," said I, giving him my hand.

He held it a moment, bowing, and looking inexpressible things.

"*Ah, Josephine*... ."

"*A demain, alors!*"

And with a simper I left my gallant and dapper cavalier to pay the bill.

CHAPTER X

RECAPTURED

At five o'clock one morning Mlle. Josephine received a staggering note from the Russian Colonel to say that he had had to leave at a moment's notice for the Caucasus, under a Turkish guard, and that there was no prospect at all of his taking his dear Josephine with him.

Thus my plan had failed. It was not the Colonel's fault, but it was annoying all the same. I had wasted both time and money, provisions and opportunities, and now I had to begin all over again.

I decided that I would not continue in my disguise as a girl. It was too nerve-racking to begin with; and also, as a girl, I could not go down myself to the docks and arrange matters at first hand. I felt I must do something for myself. During the month that had elapsed Robin had been recaptured, other officers had escaped, the whole course of the war was changing, and here was I still *embusqué* in Constantinople.

Something must be done, and, as usual, my good angel did it for me.... She bought me a small upturned moustache, spectacles, hair-dye, a second-hand suit, a stained white waistcoat which I ornamented with a large nickel gilt watch chain, a pair of old elastic-sided boots (price £7), an ebony cane with a silver top, and a bowler hat which I perched rakishly askew. I was a Hungarian mechanic, out of a job. I had lost my place at the munition factory near San Stefano. But I was not down-hearted. My nails were oily and my antecedents doubtful, but I drank my beer and smoked my cigars and looked on life brightly through my spectacles.

I did not avoid the Boche—in fact, I frequently drank beer with him. The non-Latin races are not inquisitive as a rule. They cared little whether I was Swiss or Dutch or Hungarian, and I frequently claimed all three nationalities. They did not even think it odd when, on one occasion, I said that I had been born in Scandinavia and later that I was a naturalised Hungarian, and later again (when a Jewish gentleman with military boots joined us, whom I recognised to be a Government informer, paid to pick up information) that I was really of Russian parentage and that I had a passport to this effect (which I showed to the company present) signed by Djevad Bey, the military commandant of Constantinople, permitting me to proceed to Russia and ordering that every facility should be given to me at the custom-house.

This forged passport was a source of perplexity to me at the time, and later it was to be the cause of great discomfort. I had bought it for ten pounds from the gentleman whose pumicestone engraving die reposed at the bottom of the cistern. It was an ornate affair, duly stamped, and sealed, and signed with a Turkish flourish. But I could not bring myself to believe that it would get me through the passport office, the *douane*, and the medical station at the entrance to the Bosphorus. Some hitch would certainly have occurred.

However, it impressed the company in the café. People generally take one at one's own valuation, and the few secret agents to whom I spoke obviously considered that I was not a likely person to be blackmailed. With the Greeks I was certainly popular. The seedy-smart polyglot youth who was so liberal with his cigars (which were rather a rarity then) and so fond of talking politics and drinking beer was a *persona grata* in the circles he frequented. We talked much of revolution.

"We will crucify the Young Turks," said a Greek to me one day, "and then eat them in little bits. We will——" His expressive hands suddenly paused in mid-gesture, and his mouth dropped open, but only for an instant. He had seen a detective enter. "We will continue to preserve our dignity and remain calm whatever happens," he concluded neatly.

But calm the Greeks certainly were not.

In the cellar of a German hotel in Pera the Greek proprietor displayed one night a collection of rusty swords and old revolvers which were the nucleus of the New Age of brotherly love, when the streets were to run with Turkish blood, and the Cross replace the Crescent in San Sophia. I was privileged to be present at this conclave of desperadoes. After swearing each other to eternal secrecy we sampled some of the contents of our host's cellar, and talked very big about what we were going to do. But our host, beyond dancing a hornpipe and declaring that he was going to murder everybody in the hotel (after they had paid their bills), propounded no very definite scheme.

Out of this atmosphere of melodrama one emerged into the sombre, silent streets and went rather furtively home, feeling that there was something to be said for the Turks after all. But I need hardly say that no influential Greeks had a share in these proceedings: they were always on the side of moderation. One had been a fool to consort with fools.

Behind the lattices of the harems it was said that Enver Pasha's day was done. The new Sultan had thrown him out of the palace, neck and crop. There was to be an inquiry into the means by which he had acquired huge farms round Constantinople—farms which were supposed to be purchased from the proceeds of a corner in milk that had killed many children. The Custodians of the Harem (and in Turkey these tall flat-chested individuals have positions of great power; the Chief of the White Custodians, for instance, is one of the high dignitaries of the Empire, and ranks with a Lord Chamberlain) had long been intriguing against the Committee and especially against the German element with Enver at its head.... The Sultan was high in popular favour, and a dramatic suicide in the main street of Pera, which lifted a corner of the curtain hiding the unrest behind the scenes at the Imperial Palace, became a nine days' wonder, and gave rise to extraordinary rumours. A Turkish officer in full uniform had been seen running for dear life down the Grand Rue de Pera, pursued by policemen. The officer took refuge in the Turkish club, but he was refused asylum there. The policemen crowded into the entrance hall to arrest him, while the fugitive dashed upstairs to the card-room. Finding, however, that he could not avoid arrest, he threw himself out of the window, and was instantly killed on the pavement below. For some time, the corpse, dressed in the uniform of the Yildiz Guards, blocked the traffic of the city.

A few days later a British air-raid gave the Constantinopolitans something new to think about. It was a stifling night, and I was dozing and listening to the mosquitoes that buzzed round me, when their drone seemed to grow louder and louder. I lay quite still, thinking that another raid would be too good to be true. But presently there was no doubt about it. Invisible, but very audible, the British squadron was sailing overhead. I jumped up and at that moment the Turks put up their barrage. Bang! Boom! Whizz! Kk—kk—kk! All the little voices of civilisation were speaking.

Greeks crowded into the streets, and clapped their hands when the crash and rumble of a bomb was heard in the Turkish quarter of Stamboul.

"The Sultan is going to make peace," they told me. "He has refused to gird on the Sword of Othman until the Committee of Union and Progress give an account of their funds."

"Hurrah for the English!" shouted others, quite undismayed by the shrapnel and falling pieces of shell.

Here are some chance remarks, actually heard during air raids.

"Ah! Here is the revolution at last!" said a Turkish officer in a chemist's shop in the Grand Rue de Pera, thinking the firing meant the downfall of Enver Pasha and his gang.

"Bread costs four shillings a two-pound loaf," said an Armenian in the suburb of Chichli—"and as often as not there is a stone or half a mouse thrown into the four shillings' worth, for luck. May this gang of swindlers perish!"

"Allah! send the English soon," wailed a Turkish widow in a hovel in Stamboul, where she was living with her five starving children. "We are being killed by inches now; it would be better to be killed quickly by bombs. The English cannot be worse than Enver."

This, indeed, was the general opinion in Constantinople. Few of the population, outside the high officials, bore us any grudge. The thieving of the Young Turks was on as vast a scale as their ambition. From needy adventurers they had become the prosperous potentates of an Empire. No country, surely, has ever been the prey of such desperate and determined men.

The air raids were one of the first causes of their weakening hold on the people. The moral effect of these demonstrations was incalculable, coming as it did at a time when the Sultan was supposed to be in favour of peace.

Peace, indeed, was the only faint hope of salvation that remained to the very poor. Milk had almost disappeared from the open market, and for some time past children had been exposed in the street, their mothers being unable to support them any longer.

Each night, when I passed the Petits Champs, I saw a row of starving children, poor little living protests of humanity against the barbarisms of war and the cruelty of profiteers, huddled on the pavement, mute, uncomplaining, too weak to even ask for alms.

And Bedri Bey, sometime Prefect of Police at Constantinople, when appealed to, said: "*Bah! Les pauvres, qu'ils crèvent.*"

Although politics were interesting enough, escape was my first preoccupation. It was necessary to approach the harbour officials with caution, and they, on their side, although ready enough to help with suggestions, seemed inclined to shelve all the actual work on to a person or persons unknown, who remained in the background. It was very difficult to get at the principals.

One of the chief agents of escape, however, I met one day in the Grand Rue de Pera. He was a most remarkable man. Intrigue was the breath of his nostrils, and although he had made thousands of pounds by helping rich refugees out of the country, he was really more interested in politics than pelf. He laid the groundwork of such knowledge as I acquired of Constantinople.

Incidentally, in the course of our conversation, a squad of Russian officer prisoners passed, accompanied by two sentries whom I knew quite well. So confident did I feel of not being recognised that I said a few words to one of the Russians, while their escort glanced at me with faces perfectly blank. They had not the vaguest idea who I was.

To get away from Constantinople, the escape merchant told me, was a matter of passing the custom house. Formerly this had been easy, but now every ship was searched from stem to stern and from deck to keelson. Also every skipper was a Mohammedan. All Christians had been recently deprived of their positions.

Still, Mohammedans are not an unbribable people, and something might possibly be done for me. In fact, that very day he had learnt of a certain Lazz shipmaster, who was going over to the Caucasus in his own boat, and who would be prepared to take a few passengers for a consideration.

Later in the same day I heard that two other officers, who had escaped about a week before (by bolting under a train in Haidar Pasha railway station), were already in touch with this Lazz. I went to see them early the following morning and we agreed to charter the boat between us, so as to reduce expenses.

My two friends were living in the house of one Theodore, a Greek waiter at a restaurant in Sirkedji, who believed that they, as well as myself, were Germans.

The Lazz, who came to visit us, was absolutely astounded when we proclaimed ourselves as British officers: he had been under the impression that we were some sort of Turkish subject. However, all passengers were grist to his mill, and British officers who talked glibly of gold payments were not people to be neglected. After haggling about terms, we made an appointment for the next day, and parted with some cordiality.

On the morrow, punctual to our appointments, the Lazz and I again arrived at Theodore's house to confer further with my two friends.

As it was a very hot afternoon, I took off my coat and my false moustache, before plunging into the details of our departure. It was evident that the Lazz was in a hurry to be off. His cargo was complete, he said. He had only to take in petrol for his motor before leaving on the following day. There remained the question of money, and after much argument we settled to pay him five hundred pounds on arrival at the port of Poti in the Caucasus, and one hundred pounds advance for fuel immediately. He was to provide the disguises necessary for us to pass the customs at the Bosphorus. We were each of us to don a black dress and a black veil and to sit in a row in his cabin, refusing to move or speak if interrogated. Muslim ladies, he assured us, had frequently refused to undergo any scrutiny whatever at the customs, and provided they were vouched for by some responsible person on board, the gallant excisemen were ready to let them pass. As his very own wives, said the Lazz, no harm could possibly come to us, provided of course we remained sitting, and silent, throughout the inspection.

This seemed a very satisfactory scheme, for obviously whatever risks we ran, our friend the Lazz would run them too.

By evening our pact was complete. We handed over a hundred pounds, and the Lazz promised faithfully that he would have the boat ready and our disguises prepared by nightfall on the following day, when we would sail for Russia.

Hardly had the money changed hands before I noticed a suspicious-looking individual in the street below. Presently he was joined by another detective, whom I recognised.

Things looked ugly.

We took the Lazz cautiously to the window.

"Do you know anything about those men?" we asked.

He turned deathly pale, but swore he had never seen them before. I do not think he had. His fear was genuine.

"Let me get out! Let me get out!" he said, making a bolt for the door.

And he went. There was no use in trying to stop him.

One of my friends and I now went downstairs, while the third member of our party stayed behind to hide a few odds and ends of gear, in case the house was searched.

We waited downstairs, making light of our fears, and fighting a premonition of disaster.

Presently there was a loud tapping on the door. Even if it were the police, I thought, our disguises would carry us through. Then I noticed that my friend was in shirt-sleeves. I put on my spectacles and tried to stick on my moustache again, but the gum from it had gone.

The rapping at the door became louder and louder, and presently it was opened by a flustered female.

In trooped six detectives, including the man I had recognised, who was apparently their leader.

"There are some British officers hiding here," he said fiercely to the woman; "show me where they are."

While this scene was passing in the entrance-hall, we were behind the door of the pantry.

A detective came in and caught my friend. Meanwhile two others were pommelling the unfortunate woman to make her say where we were. She kept pleading that she knew nothing about any British officers.

Another instant, and I should have been found. So I came out from behind the pantry door, and crossed the entrance hall.

In the doorway stood a burly policeman, who said "*Yok, yok*," when I attempted to pass him.

Had I had the requisite nerve I believe I could have bluffed this man. Some phrase with *schweinhund* in it would probably have got me past. But I hesitated, and was lost.

My hand flew to my breast pocket, where the forged passport lay, and my false moustache.

"Seize that man and search him," said the head detective, looking over the banisters. Then he went upstairs, dragging the woman with him.

My arms were instantly caught from behind, while a seedy-looking youth, who was probably a pick-pocket in his spare time, ran his fingers over my clothes. My wad of money, watch, compass, passport, moustache, everything was put into a small canvas bag, and I was then taken to the opposite corner of the room to that in which my friend sat, and told not to move under pain of death. A levelled revolver emphasised the injunction.

THE AUTHOR AS A HUNGARIAN MECHANIC

Presently there were cries of women heard from the attic, then there was a loud crash, and I knew that the third member of our party had fallen through the trapdoor leading to the roof.

That was the last of my freedom for the time. Thus suddenly my five weeks' scheming was ended.

Each of us was taken charge of by two policemen, who linked their arms in ours. Presently the order to march was given, and a dismal procession, consisting of two weeping women, a seedy-smart individual in a bowler hat, two youths in slippers and shirt-sleeves, and a Greek waiter, could be seen wending their way to the Central Gaol of Stamboul.

CHAPTER XI

THE BLACK HOLE OF CONSTANTINOPLE

Before leaving, we had protested strongly against the treatment of the women in the house.

"But they are Turkish subjects," said the detectives.

"Anyway, they are women," we protested.

But this had little effect. Theodore and his unfortunate family were marched off behind us to the Central Gaol. I think, however, that our protest was not quite in vain, for it gave the women courage. When I last saw them, before being taken to the Chief of Police, they had dried their tears. Eventually they were released, but not, alas! until they had endured much suffering.

The Chief of Police congratulated us on being safe once more in Turkish hands.

"Yes, we are comfortably back in prison," I said with a faint smile, "and therefore there is surely no harm in giving us back the personal trifles that the detectives took from us."

"I cannot give you your papers," he said. "There is a forged passport here, amongst other things."

"Very well, do as you like about that," I said, shrugging my shoulders, "but surely my empty pocket-book and my watch might be returned."

To this he agreed, whereupon he handed me—

(a) My pocket-book, containing five pounds hidden in the lining.

(b) My watch, and a compass, which he mistook for another timepiece.

(c) My false moustache, which had been captured on my person.

I was in an agony of anxiety about this moustache. Had the police inquired at the only two hairdressers' where such things were made, they would have found that Miss Whitaker had ordered it for me only ten days before. But now it was safely in my possession again. I had the only connecting link of evidence that might incriminate Miss Whitaker in my trouser pocket, and was tearing it to shreds as I talked to the Chief of Police.

The interview passed on a note of felicitation, until the very end. After praising the smart way his men had surrounded the house, and receiving his congratulations on our escapes, just as if the whole thing was a game, we said that there was one criticism we had to make on police methods, and that was their treatment of women.

"They are Turkish subjects," snapped the Chief of Police, suddenly showing his teeth.

"They are women," we retorted, "and they are innocent. If they are maltreated ____"

"I know how to manage my affairs," he said with a gasp of annoyance.

"Certainly. But if they are maltreated you will be responsible after the war."

To this he made no reply.

We were removed without further ado, and after being photographed and measured in the most approved fashion for criminals, we were taken up long flights of stairs, and across a roof, to the quarters for prisoners awaiting trial. Here we were allotted separate cells, where we were to pass the next few days in strict isolation.

To my amazement (for I knew something of Turkish prisons from a previous experience, not here recorded) these cells were scrupulously clean. A bed, a table, and a chair were in each apartment, all very firm and foursquare, as if designed to withstand any access of fury or despair on the prisoner's part. There was electric light in the ceiling, covered with wire netting. Walls and woodwork were of a neutral colour. The windows, which were barred, had a convenient arrangement for regulating the ventilation. The heavy door, which admitted no sound, was provided with a sliding hatch, which could be opened by the warders at will for purposes of investigation. Everything was hideously efficient.

Turkey is a country of surprises, but I was not prepared for this. I would have preferred something more picturesque. One's mind, after the testing climax of recapture, craves for new doses of excitement.

The brain of a criminal, after he has been apprehended, must be a turmoil of thought. He curses his stupidity, or his luck, or his associates. He longs to explain and defend himself. Instead of this, he is left in silence in a drab room, with no company but his thoughts.

My own thoughts were most unpleasant. I had failed miserably and innocent people were suffering as the result.

After five weeks of effort I was farther than ever from escape. Worse than all, Miss Whitaker was in danger. Never again shall I pass such dismal hours. I see myself now, seated on that solid chair with head on arms, bent over that efficient table. A prisoner's heart must soon turn to stone.

But although our surroundings were inhuman, one of our gaolers had a generous heart. He opened the slot in my door merely to say he was sorry about it all, and that the women were all right. It is little actions such as these that so often light the darkest hours of life. The man was a European Turk.

It was urgently necessary to communicate with my fellow-prisoners, in order to arrange to tell the same story. My friend next door solved the problem by bawling up through his barred window at the top of his voice that he would leave a note for me in the wash-place.

"Right you are!" I howled in answer, and instantly the slot of my door opened, and I had to explain that I was singing.

Already, interest was beginning to creep back into one's life. I found the note in the wash-place, read it secretly, thought over my answer, and transcribed the message on to a cigarette paper. Having no writing material, I used the end of a match dipped into an ink prepared from tobacco juice and ash. By these simple means we established a regular means of communication and before forty-eight hours of our strict seclusion had elapsed we were all three in possession of a complete, circumstantial, and fictitious account of our adventures prior to capture.

When not engaged on reminiscences, I was generally pacing my cell, or trying to invent some new form of exercise to keep myself fit. But at times energy failed and one felt inclined to gnash one's teeth at the futility of it all.

One day, when I was feeling inclined to gnash my teeth, the slot in my door was furtively withdrawn, and, instead of a gaoler, a very comely vision appeared at the observation hatch. A pair of laughing black eyes were looking in on me. She wrinkled her nose, and laughed. I jumped up, thinking I was dreaming, and hoping that the dream would continue. At the same moment something dropped on to my floor. Then the trap door was softly shutto.

I found a tiny stump of lead pencil. That was proof of the reality of my vision.

Countless excuses to leave my cell, and voluminous correspondence with the pencil's aid eventually enabled me to find out that she was an Armenian girl, awaiting trial, who took a deep interest in us. At great risk to herself, she had provided the three of us with writing instruments. Except for a brief glimpse, and a mumbled word, I was never able to thank her, however, owing to circumstances beyond our control.

On the fourth day we were transferred to the Military Prison in the Square of the Seraskerat.

As usual in Turkey, our move was sudden and unexpected. That morning, on complaining at mid-day that I had as yet received no food, I was told that *inshallah*—if God pleased—it would arrive in due course.

Instead of a belated breakfast, however, a *posse* of policemen arrived, and we started on our journeys again: my friends still in their shirt-sleeves and slippers, and myself still in my bowler hat, although I did not now wear it so rakishly.

But we were fairly cheery. We had learnt (no matter how) that the females of Theodore's family would soon be released, and that Theodore himself, although still in duress, would not suffer any extreme fate. Also, it was by now fairly obvious that Miss Whitaker would not be apprehended, as sufficient evidence was not obtainable against her. She had covered her tracks too well. All things considered, there was no cause for depression.

But waiting is hungry work. That afternoon still saw us, fretful and unfed, waiting outside the office of Djevad Bey, the Military Commandant of Constantinople.

At last I was taken into an ornate room, where I had my first talk with this redoubtable individual, who was popularly supposed to be the hangman of the Young Turks. Anyone less like an executioner I have never seen. He was plump, well-dressed, with humorous grey eyes. He wore long, rather well-fitting boots, and smoked his cigarettes from a long amber holder. He also had a long amber moustache, which was being trained Kaiser-wise.

I stood before him at attention.

"About this forged passport," he began—"do gentlemen in your country forge each other's signatures?"

"It is not usual," I admitted.

"Then you, as an English gentleman, surely did not counterfeit my writing?"

"Oh no! I wouldn't dream of doing such a thing."

"Then how do you account for this passport being in your possession?"

I remained silent.

"Who forged it?" he insisted.

"May I look?" said I. "Is that really your signature?"

"It is indeed. With it you could easily have got out of the country."

"What an idiot I was not to use it!" I said with quite unfeigned annoyance.

"You were!" he laughed—"they would have passed you straight through the

Customs on seeing this."

I felt very faint at this moment, and staggered against the table. But I recovered after an instant. I quite forget his next few remarks, but I know that I committed myself to a story that I had bought the passport from a man in a restaurant whom I could not now recognise.

"But where have you been living all these weeks?" he asked.

"I was living in the ruins near the Fatih mosque," I said glibly—"and I used to lunch and dine at various cafés in the city, a different one every day. It was in one of these places that I bought the passport."

Djevad Bey considered this statement for a moment. There was a nasty look in his eye when he spoke again.

"I shall never rest until I know who it is who can forge my signature so well," he said—"and until I know, I am afraid you will be very uncomfortable, for by law you are in the position of a common malefactor."

"By law I am in the position of a prisoner of war," I answered—"and as such, I am liable to a fortnight's simple imprisonment, for attempting to escape. The Turkish Government signed this agreement only a few months ago with the British representatives at Berne."

"A man who forges another's name is not an officer, but a forger," he said meaningly.

"Say what you like, and do what you like," I answered—"I am in your power. But one thing I ask, and that is, that if you punish me, you should liberate the innocent Theodore and his family. True, we were found in their house, but ─────"

"I cannot believe what you say," said Djevad Bey thoughtfully.

There was a pause. Then:

"Come, as man to man, won't you tell me who forged that passport?"

"You have just called me a liar," said I. "That ends the matter."

And with an all-is-over-between-us air I left the room, feeling dizzy and uncomfortable.

It was then four o'clock in the afternoon, and I had not yet eaten. I did not feel at all amused at the prospect of the Military Prison.

I was taken downstairs into the darkness, on entering this inferno of the damned of Enver Pasha. There were cries and shouts down there, and men scrambling for food, and other men who looked like wild animals, behind bars. A swarthy custodian took my name, and I then proceeded, down a long corridor, until my escort reached an iron portal such as Dante imagined long ago.

Lasciate ogni speranza voi ch'entrate... . The gates had clanged behind me, and I was in a long, low room below ground level, airless, ill-lit, filthy with tomato skins and bits of bread. Well-fed rats were scurrying amongst the garbage, and badly-fed prisoners were pacing the room forlornly, or twiddling their thumbs, or scratching themselves, or gnawing crusts of bread.

They gathered round me, clamouring for news and cigarettes. In less than no time they had picked my pockets. They had no more morals than monkeys. Poor devils! who could blame them, living as they did down there, where no rumours are heard of the outside world, except the cries of beaten men and the dull sound of wood on flesh?

"What are you in for?" they asked me.

"Forgery," said I, not to be outdone by any desperado present.

One man, however, confessed to murder, having cut a small boy's throat a few months before. With him I could not compete. But the most of us were fraudulent contractors, spies, petty swindlers and the like. Our morals, as I have said, were practically *nil*. Yet I noticed that a Jew lived quite apart, and was shunned by everybody. By trade he was a brigand, but this was no slur on his character as a criminal: the failing that had led to ostracism was that he pilfered the other prisoners' tomatoes. That was really beyond a joke... .

One of my newly found friends took me to a bed, consisting of two planks on an iron frame, which he said I could have for my very, very own. He also gave me a piece of bread and some water. On beginning to eat I at once realised how hungry I was, and inquired how I should obtain further nourishment.

"Luxuries are very difficult to obtain," he said; "how much money have you got?"

"Twenty-five piastres,[9]" I answered.

He pulled a long face.

"That won't go far. But every evening at eight a boy comes round with the scraps left over from the Officers' Restaurant. Otherwise you will live on bread and tomatoes."

"What about bedding?" I asked, to change the subject.

"Bedding!" he said, looking at me as if I was a perfect idiot. "Do you mean to say you have come here without any bedding?"

I admitted I had, but felt too exhausted to explain.

One was utterly lost in that dungeon. Even when the war ended, would one be found? I doubted it. Yet as I would naturally never reveal the forger's name, it seemed unlikely that I would get out… . Then I thought of my companions. I imagined them happily together, in some place where one could see the sky… . As for me, I might languish down here for ever. Obviously something should be done.

But what? I rose (rather hastily, for on looking between the planks of my bed, I noticed that the crack was entirely filled with battalions of board beasts in line, waiting for a night attack), and began to pace our narrow and nasty apartment. A group of prisoners were cooking some pitiful mess by the window. Four others played poker with a very greasy pack. One was twiddling his thumbs very fast, and I suddenly recollected that he had been twiddling his thumbs very fast half an hour ago, when I had first seen him. The lonely Jew was removing lice from the seams of his coat, and throwing his quarry airily about the room.

Then I noticed that besides ourselves, there were other prisoners even more unfortunate. There had been so much to see in my new surroundings that I had not noticed the people in chains… . One side of our room opened out on to some half-dozen cubicles, each of which contained a prisoner in chains. These cells had no light or ventilation. They measured six feet in length by four in breadth. In solitude and obscurity, fettered by wrist and ankle to shackles that weighed a hundredweight, human beings lived there—and are still living for aught I know—for months and even years, until death released them. These men were ravenous and verminous, but they had by no means lost their hope and faith. I shall never hear the hymn—

> "Thy rule, O Christ, begin,
> Break with Thine iron rod
> The tyrannies of sin …"

without remembering that an Armenian lad said those words to me, lying in chains in one of these cells. With another prisoner, a Greek, who had endured eleven months of this torture, I also had some speech.

"Yes, the war will be over soon," he said. "My God, how good this cigarette of yours tastes! I haven't touched tobacco for a month. But be careful. The sentries must not see you speaking to me."

"Yes, the chains were bad at first," he continued when the sentry's back was turned, "but one gets used to anything in time. And I have had time enough. It takes a lot to kill a healthy man. Before I came in here I used to be strong and well. I used to ride two hours every day, on my own horses. Now my horses have gone to feed the Turkish Army and I can hardly drag my chains as far as the water-tap. But God is great... ."

God is great! *Allahu akbar!*

I determined to get away from that dungeon at all costs, if for no other reason than because I had to survive to write about it.

I went to the big gate, and tried to bluff the sentry to let me go to see the Commandant. But a clean face and a full stomach are practically necessary to a *débonnaire* appearance. When one is scrubby and starved it is almost impossible to succeed in "wangling." I stared at the sentry through my eyeglass, and I offered him my twenty-five piastres as if I had plenty more *baksheesh* to give to a good boy, but I utterly and dismally failed to impress him.

"*Yok, yok, yok,*" he said, looking at me as one might look at an orang-outang that has

DO NOT IRRITATE THIS ANIMAL

written over its cage.

I gibbered in impotent rage, and then went and put my head under a tap.

A little later, while I was drying my head with my handkerchief, I saw some barbers come to the big gate. They stood there, clapping and clacking their strops. Instantly, my fellow-prisoners rushed to the gate as if they had heard the beating of the wings of some angel of deliverance. This was apparently the occasion of their weekly shave, when egress to the corridor was permitted, the barbers naturally not wishing to go inside our loathsome room.

Taking this tide in the affairs of men at the flood, I found it led on to fortune. I was in the corridor with six other prisoners, and a barber confronted me with a razor in his hand. He whetted his steel expectantly, but I would have none of him, and seized a passing official by the arm.

He was a dog-collar gentleman.

A dog-collar gentleman, I must explain, is Authority Incarnate. On his swelling chest he wears a crescent tablet of brass, with the one word *Quanun* inscribed thereon. *Quanun* means "law," and the wearer of this badge is responsible for public decorum of every kind. If a Turkish officer be seen drinking alcohol in uniform, or playing cards, or flirting, or talking disrespectfully of the Germans, or indulging in any other prohibited amusement, he is instantly arrested by the dog-collar gentleman, and brought to prison. In his official capacity, the dog-collar gentleman is one of the most important personages in Turkey: policeman, pussfoot and prude in one.

"There is some mistake," I said excitedly. "I am a British officer, and have been put in a room with criminals."

"You a British officer?" said the dog-collar man incredulously.

"A captain of cavalry," said I, slipping him the twenty-five piastre note.

"*Pekke, Effendim*," he answered. "Very good, sir, I will see what can be done."

I had burnt my boats now.

About ten minutes later, just as I was flatly refusing to either be shaved or to return through the gate, a sergeant-major and a squad of soldiers arrived and bore me off to the Prison Commandant.

Here I caught sight of my two companions, and was able to fling them a few words through the "Yok, yok" of the sentries. They also had been separated, and put amongst criminals. Their lot had been no different to mine.

"A slight mistake has occurred," said the Prison Commandant to me, "but now you shall have one of the best rooms in the prison. Only I am afraid you will be alone there, until after your trial."

Of course I did not believe him, but I was glad that I was to be alone.

I was taken to a room on the upper floor, furnished with a bed and blanket, and with a window opening on to a corridor, where people were always passing. The Commandant had spoken the truth. It was quite a good room, as prison apartments go, and the traffic of the corridor amused me.

At nine o'clock that night I was able to get a dish of haricot beans, my first meal of the day.

Then I settled down to a month of solitary confinement.

I think I may claim to write of this torture, which exists not only in Turkey but through the prisons of the civilised world, with some expert knowledge. I use the word "torture" because it is nothing less. Solitary confinement is a punishment as barbarous and as senseless as the thumbscrew or the rack: more so indeed, for it is better to kill the body than to maim the mind. The spirit of man is more than his poor flesh; the war has reminded us of that. And if it has also reminded us that our prison systems are archaic, so much the better for the world.

At times, in gaol, a tide of pity rose in me for all life created that is caged by man.

Take a felon at one end of the scale, and a canary at the other. The felon is imprisoned for twenty years. For twenty years, less some small remission for good conduct, an abnormal brain lives in abnormal surroundings, where hope dies, and ideals fail. He has sinned against society, and therefore society murders his mind. Corporal and capital punishment, I have come to believe, are saner than the cruelties, immeasurable by "the world's coarse thumb and finger," suffered by the mind of man in solitary confinement or the common gaol. The sentimentalist who shudders at the cat and gallows forgets the worse, slow, hidden horrors that pass unseen in the felon's brain. Perhaps the sentimentalist does not realise them. Perhaps also the old lady who keeps a canary does not realise the feelings of her pet. She may think she is protecting it from the birds and beasts outside. But I feel now that I know what the canary feels... . However, it is difficult to argue about questions involving imagination.

I lived on hope, chiefly, during the days that followed. With nothing to read, no cutting instrument of any sort, no washing arrangements, and no one to speak to, the time passed hideously. I used to gaze at my watch sometimes, appalled at the slow passage of time. The second-hand had a horrible fascination for me. It simply crawled round its dial and each instant, between the jerks of the little hand, the precious moments of my youth were passing, beyond recall. Madness lay that way. If I had been a real criminal, I wondered, would I have repented? Unquestionably the answer was, "No!" Solitary confinement would have made me a permanent enemy of society.

There were no smiles and soap in that Military Prison, no scissors, no sanitation. There was nothing human or clean about it. Nothing but destruction will rid it of its vermin, or scour it of its taint of disease and death.

Perhaps the lack of scissors was the amenity of life whose absence I most deplored. Try to do without a cutting instrument for a month, and you will realise why it was that some sort of cutting edge was the first need of primitive man and remains a prime necessity to-day.

However, as a matter of fact, I did not remain a whole month without a cutting edge. Before a fortnight had elapsed I had bettered my position in many ways. I had secured a knife (which I stole from the restaurant), a wash-basin (sent from the Embassy), and pencil and paper from a friendly clerk. With these writing instruments I used to correspond voluminously with the other British prisoners, by various privy methods.

I had a regular routine for my days now. Early mornings were devoted to walking briskly up and down my room in various gaits—the sailor's roll, for instance, and the Napoleonic stride, and the deportment of various of my acquaintances. During this time I avoided thinking, but generally imagined some incident in which I took a distinguished part. In the forenoon I played games, such as throwing my soap to the ceiling and catching it again, or juggling with cigarettes, both lighted and unlighted. The afternoon generally passed in sleep, but the evening and nights were bad. It was then that the second hand of my watch began to exert its fascination. The electric light bulb, however, could occasionally be tampered with, and on these occasions there was always the hope that the sentries would get a shock in putting it right. Also I found amusement in my watch chain, which I made into an absorbing puzzle.

But, curiously enough, I found it impossible to write anything, except lengthy letters.

A real prisoner in a well-constituted prison does not enjoy his days any more than I did. On the other hand, he knows how long his sentence is going to last, whereas in my case I was confined during Djevad Bey's pleasure, or the duration of the war, and each day brought me nearer nothing—except insanity.

One evening, however, an Imperial Son-in-law entered my room, and lit my life with a certain interest. His father, who was a Court official, had betrothed him to a princess, and he had consequently assumed the title of Damad, or Son-in-law. This youth had had a remarkable career. While still a guileless lad, scarcely broke from the harem, he had used his revolver so injudiciously that he had seriously damaged one of the Imperial apartments, besides killing the elderly Colonel at whom he was aiming. Enver Pasha had of course himself a weakness for this sort of thing, but still, to save appearances, the Damad had to be punished. He was therefore condemned to three months' confinement in the Military Prison. Although nominally in residence there, he used, however, to leave prison every Friday to attend the Sultan's Selamlik, and only return on Monday night. Moreover, he not only thoroughly amused himself during his protracted week-ends, he also squeezed every bit of pleasure possible out of his prison days. Life was a lemon, which he sucked with grace. He was free to wander where he wished in the prison, and to eat and drink what he liked. The best of everything was good enough for the Damad. Grapes came for him from the Sultan's garden, and a faithful negro slave was always at his heels.

The Damad had rather charming manners. He knocked politely before entering my cell.

"Excuse my interrupting," he said, "but——"

"You are not interrupting me at all," I answered, getting up from my bed. "I do wish you would stop and talk. Have a cigarette? I haven't talked to anyone for a fortnight."

"I am so sorry, but I daren't talk to you. That is a pleasure to come. I wanted to borrow something, that's all. And, I say, will you allow me to offer you one of my cigarettes—they're the Sultan's brand, you know. Better take the box. Well, I saw you with an eyeglass through the window in the passage. Will you lend it me to appear at the next Selamlik?"

I was delighted, and said so. To my sorrow, the Damad instantly took his departure.

"Smuggle me in something to read," I said, as he left with profuse apologies for his hurry.

He nodded, and his long left eyelash flickered.

Next day his little nigger boy, when the sentry's back was turned, popped about twenty leaflets into my window. I seized them avidly, and found that they were the astounding adventures of Nat Pinkerton in French. Never have my eyes rested so gleefully on a printed page. I consumed them cautiously, else I should have gorged myself with excitement at a single sitting. Like an epicure, I made them last, by always breaking off at the critical juncture of the great detective's affairs. From that moment my life flowed in more agreeable channels.

"Devouring time, blunt though the lion's paws." ... I suddenly understood Shakespeare's meaning afresh. Time had dulled the clawing of regret.

I had failed to escape, it is true, but there was always hope. Things were getting better. The women had been released. Thémistoclé only awaited a formal trial. My own condition had improved. I had been moved from my solitary confinement, just when I had secured a Bible, and a large tin of Keating's, wherewith to combat the devils of captivity. But any change is better than none at all, I thought. The mortal hunger for companionship is strong, and my new room, besides containing an officer, also enjoyed an excellent and varied view.

After a few days' experience of my new room-mate, however, who was a Bulgarian Bolshevik, I began to pine for solitude again. A more unmitigated Tishbite I have never seen, but fortunately he was smaller than I. When I found him washing his feet in my basin one night, I smote him, hip and thigh.

That Bulgarian has coloured my whole view of the Balkans. The less said about him, the better.

One day about thirty British officers arrived from the camp at Yuzgad, whence they had escaped and been recaptured on the occasion when Commander Cochrane and his gallant band of seven marched four hundred and fifty miles to freedom. All the party who arrived in the Military Prison were in uniform, and in excellent spirits. They were like a breath of fresh air in that sordid place. On being put into three rooms, these thirty brave men and true at once demanded beds to sleep on. In due time the beds arrived, in the usual condition of beds in that place. They might have been so many Stilton cheeses. Our thirty prisoners, despite the protest of the guards, carried out their couches into the passage, and lit two Primus stoves. Over these stoves they proceeded to pass the component parts of each bed, so that its occupants were utterly exterminated.

Imagine the scene. A dismal corridor, a flaming stove, Turkish sentries protesting with Hercules in khaki, cleansing the Augean stable.... But protests were useless. The smell of burnt bugs mingled with the other contaminations of the prison. Our officers had done in little what civilisation will one day do at large throughout that land.

A British officer, going to the feeding place, looked into a window which gave on to my room. But I was kept strictly apart from my fellows, and the sentry consequently tried to drag the officer away.

"Leave me alone, you son of Belial!" said he. "Isn't a window meant to look through?"

Windows in that prison were certainly not meant to look through.

From my new eyrie I had a composite view of startling contrasts. Down below, some soldiers were living in a verandah, behind wooden bars. Anything more animal than their life it would be impossible to conceive. Every afternoon at three o'clock a parade of handcuffed men were marshalled two by two, and then pushed into these dens. Beyond them lay the city of Stamboul with its clustered cupolas and nine-trellised alley-ways. And beyond the city were the blue waters of the Marmora.

Then there was the window in the passage through which the British officer had observed me. This gave me a view of the rank and fashion of the prison, so that I knew who was being tried, who received visitors, and so on.

And directly opposite me, in another face of the building, was yet another window, with curtains drawn. That was the window of the Hall of Justice. Directly under my perch, but rather too far to jump, were some telegraph lines which might possibly have provided a means of escape. Sentries used to watch me carefully, whenever I looked at these telegraph lines. I was considered a dangerous, indeed a desperate character, and my every movement was regarded with apprehension. Not only was no one (except now the Bulgarian) allowed to speak to me, but I was not even permitted to look at anything, or anyone, for long, without being bidden to desist. Whatever I did, in fact, I was told not to do.

Eventually I made a scene.

The immediate cause of the row was that I had a glimpse of a sitting in the Hall of Justice. I had often wondered what passed there, for at times faint screams used to hint of the infamies that passed behind those curtains.

One day I saw.

The Hall of Justice is a fine room, with a lordly sweep of view over the city and the sea. Why anyone chose such a situation as a torture chamber I do not know. But there it was. There was something dramatic about the beautiful prospect and the bestial people who sat with their backs turned to it, interrogating the Armenians.

"Every prospect pleases and only man is vile."

Very vile were the two Turkish officers, judges I suppose, who sat smoking cigarettes, while an old Armenian woman and her son stood before them to be tried. What passed I could not hear, but evidently her answers were not satisfactory, for presently the policeman who stood behind her kicked her violently, so that her head jerked back and her arms flung forward, and she was sent tottering towards the judges' table. Then the policeman took a stick as thick as a man's wrist, and began to beat her over the head and shoulders. Her son meanwhile had fallen on his knees and was crawling about the room, dragging his chains, and supplicating first the judges and then the policeman. He was imploring them, no doubt, to have pity on his mother's age and weakness.

She fell down in a faint. The policeman kicked her in the face, and then prodded her with a stick until she rose.

I wish the people who are ready to "let the Turk manage his own country" could have seen that savage pantomime.

I tried to get out to stop it, but was driven back with bayonets.

Djevad Bey, the Military Commandant of Constantinople, with a resplendent retinue, arrived one day to inspect us. With his long cigarette-holder, and long shiny boots, he swaggered round, followed by *ormulu* staff officers and diligent clerks and pompous gentlemen in dog-collars. Everywhere around him was dirt, disease, destitution, and despair. But Djevad Bey in his shiny boots "cared for none of these things." He was himself, with his medals and moustaches, and that was enough.

"What more do you want, *effendi*?" he asked me after I had made a few casual complaints (for it was useless to take him seriously). "You have one of the most beautiful views in Europe from the garden."

"But I am not allowed into the garden."

"Have a little patience, *mon cher*," said he. "It is rather crowded with older prisoners now. But in a little time perhaps, when I have discovered the name of that forger …"

And with a condescending smile he passed on between ranks of sentries standing stiffly at attention, to inspect another portion of his miserable menagerie.

Ah, Djevad, *mon cher*, those days seem distant now! You and your popinjays have passed... .

[9] Five shillings.

CHAPTER XII

OUR SECOND ESCAPE

The ghosts of the prisoners of the Tower, or of the Bastille, could they revisit earth, would undoubtedly have found themselves more at home in the Military Prison, Constantinople, than anywhere else in the world. The dark ages were still a matter of actuality in the dark dungeons of Constantinople in 1918. To be tried, for instance, was there considered something very up-to- date. Most prisoners were not tried, until their sentence was nearly over, when they were formally liberated.

After a month of solitary confinement, and a week of confinement with the Bulgarian, which was an even worse travail of the spirit, I received the joyful news that the preliminaries for my court-martial were almost complete.

I attended this first sitting with the thrill of a debutante going to a ball. I determined to make up arrears of talk. And I did. I began at the beginning of my life, sketched my education, and came by easy stages to my career as an officer in the Indian Cavalry. The clerk who recorded my evidence wrote for two hours without pause or intermission, but it is worthy of record that at the end of that time we had only reached the point where an officer of the Psamattia fire brigade, hearing, as I thought, a suspicious movement on the roof of the house across the street, kept a stern and steadfast gaze in our direction, while we crouched trembling under cover of the parapet. At this point the proceedings were adjourned.

But the Court had let fall a useful piece of information. Robin was back in prison, but was being kept even more secret and secluded than I.

However, love laughs at locksmiths, and it takes more than a Turkish sentry to defeat a persevering prisoner. We sighted each other in passages, we met in wash-places, we flipped notes to each other in bits of bread, or sent them by a third party concealed in cigarettes. By such means, I learnt Robin's remarkable story.... After being caught at Malgara, ten days after his first escape, he was taken back to the Central Gaol, where he was treated as a Turkish deserter and given nothing but black bread to eat. He thereupon went on hunger strike for three days, and alarmed the Turks by nearly dying in their hands. Later he was allowed to purchase a liberal diet, including even wine and cigars, which he declared were necessary to his health, but his constitution being enfeebled by privation, he developed alarming swellings over his face and scalp, which were probably due to some noxious ingredient of the hair-dye he had used. In this condition he was sent to hospital, and from hospital he escaped again. A Greek patient was his accomplice.

Giving this man ten pounds to buy a disguise with, he made an appointment with him for nine o'clock outside the German Embassy (!) and then set out on his adventures dressed in a white night-shirt. How he eluded the sentries is a mystery to me, although I inspected the place after the armistice. Patients were then saying (Turks, who are sometimes sportsmen, among them): "Here is where a British officer escaped. Thus and thus did he climb—past the sentries—along that buttress—down into the street hard by the guard-house!".... He arrived punctually at nine o'clock at the German Embassy, in his night-shirt. But the Greek accomplice was not there. He was at that moment drinking and dicing with Robin's money. For half an hour Robin waited for him by a tree in the shadows of a side street leading to the sea. The few people who passed him stared hard, and then moved nervously across to the other pavement. They thought he was a madman.

Robin, I think, felt he was a madman too. In his present situation and dress, detection was only a matter of time. However, chance might be kind and send him a disguise. Cold and disconsolate, he ascended the main road that led to the top of the Grand Rue de Pera, and taking his way through the traffic, dipped down into the ruins beyond. The saint who protects prisoners must have guided that tall white figure, that paddled across the busy town.... And more, once he was hiding in the ruins, the saint must have sent along the small boy who passed close to him in that lonely spot of cypresses and desolation. All-unknowing of the fate that awaited him behind the angle of the wall, the small boy strode sturdily along, thinking perhaps of the nice bran- bread and synthetic coffee that awaited him for supper. Robin pounced out of the shadow, and seized him by the scruff of the neck.... The victim instantly began to blubber.

"Give me all your clothes," said Robin.

"Who are you?" sobbed the little boy.

"Brigand," said Robin shortly.

This answer had the desired effect. The youth dried his tears, and divested himself of his apparel, which Robin immediately put on. The boots were much too small to wear and were returned. Still, the brigand was so satisfied with his clothes that he gave the small boy four pounds with a magnanimous gesture. Then he set out to seek his fortune, wearing a tiny fezz, and a coat whose sleeves reached half-way down his forearm. For four days he dodged about the city, never more than a few hours at one place, until, just when his strength and his funds were exhausted, he found a house to give him shelter.

From here he made a plan to escape, but was recaught through treachery at the docks, and taken back to the Military Prison. Only an Ali Baba could do justice to these experiences. Alas! the best books of adventure are just those which are never written.

Anyway we were together again, two desperadoes in dungeon, "apart but not afar."

The Damad's little nigger boy often contributed to our schemes for communication. This lad, who was in training for the position of keeper of the harem, and consequently belonged to the species that rises to eminence in Turkey, was a remarkable child. He did exactly what he liked and no one dared interfere with the little Lord Chamberlain *in posse*. He had an uncanny brain and uncanny strength, and I can quite understand the reliance which Turkish Pashas are wont to repose in these servants. I relied on him myself at times, and was never disappointed.

The arrival of a neutral Red Cross delegate, at about this time, did much to secure us better treatment. For over five weeks now I had not breathed fresh air, but directly the Red Cross delegate arrived I was allowed to go to the bath, escorted by two dog-collar gentlemen with revolvers and two sentries with side arms. While glad to feel I was employing so many of the Turkish Army while at my ablutions, I could not but deplore their anxiety on my behalf.

"No officer has ever succeeded in escaping from this wonderful gaol of yours," I said to the Prison Commandant, who (in contrast to Djevad) was quite a good fellow in his way "and I don't suppose anyone ever will. Why therefore go to the trouble of guarding us so closely? It would be a very graceful act on your part if you allowed us to go occasionally into the garden."

"Yarin, inshallah," murmured the Commandant, meaning, "To-morrow, please God."

And to-morrow, strange to say, actually arrived in about a week's time.

Perhaps a bomb raid hastened matters, by stimulating the Commandant's desire to do graceful acts before the war was over.

One of the bombs of this raid dropped in the school playground just outside the Seraskerat Square, and shattered all the windows in my passage. Fortunately all the children were away, it being Friday. No one was killed by that bomb, but a large handsome Turkish officer prisoner standing beside me in the passage, when some panes of glass beside us burst, threw himself on the floor and refused to rise again, declaring he was killed. A full ten minutes he lay, with his moustaches in the dust, surrounded by sentries. In the confusion that ensued Robin cleverly slipped over to me and we had a very useful chat.

The first and most vital thing to do, we decided, was to get into Constantinople, in order to learn how the situation really stood, and make our plans for escaping, so that in the event of our success we should be in possession of knowledge useful to the Allies.

Having settled this, we returned to our respective cells, where I witnessed a scene that, by contrast with the behaviour of the nervous Turkish officer, reminded me of the "patient deep disdain" that the East will always feel for the marvels of our age of steel. Our machines are things of a day, but the ancient needs remain. The bomb that had dropped in the playground had wrecked a large tree that stood in its centre, and hardly had its smoke cleared away before an elderly peasant appeared with a donkey and started collecting twigs and splinters for firewood. Slowly and stolidly, under that barrage-riven sky, the old man continued gathering the aftermath of the raid, before the raid was finished. Empires might crumble to the dust: he would cook his dinner with the pieces.

This bombing business "cleared the air" for us greatly, and another little incident clinched matters.

An officious sentry, who had received the usual orders about treating Robin with especial severity, so far exceeded his instructions as to slap Robin in the face when he was merely standing at the door of his room. Robin instantly knocked him down with a hook on the point of the jaw that would have sent a prizefighter to sleep, let alone a *posta*. There was a click of rifles and a glitter of bayonets. Sergeants were whistled for. Swords and spurs rang down the corridor. The Commandant arrived.

What seemed an awkward situation for Robin at first now turned greatly to his advantage. He demanded an apology from the Minister of War, and although he did not receive this, our treatment immediately improved. The Turkish sentry was so clearly in the wrong that the Commandant felt he should do something to placate us.

One day, Robin and I were told that we would be allowed into Constantinople to shop, provided we gave our parole not to escape while in the town.

This we immediately decided to do, and wrote a promise stating that while we could give no permanent engagement about our behaviour while guarded in prison, if we were allowed out into the town we bound ourselves to return faithfully to our quarters at a fixed time. Next day, accordingly, we dressed in the quaint apologies for clothes in our possession, and sallied out, blinking in the sunlight of the square.

Imagine our surprise when we found an escort of ten armed men, who were to accompany us to see that we kept our word. Highly incensed, we returned directly to the Commandant's office, followed by our retinue. At first the Commandant did not understand the nature of the insult he had offered to us, but eventually he agreed that a squad of soldiers was unnecessary to enforce an Englishman's promise, and he promised to send us out again on the following day, more suitably attended.

This time there were only two dog-collar gentlemen to accompany us, and although we were later joined by a third, who, I think, smelt beer and beef in the offing, we considered that this number of attendants was not unsuitable to our importance. (For a long time after escape, indeed, I was always expecting to find a sentry at my elbow. They were very convenient for carrying parcels, and during this excursion the minions of the law actually carried back to prison our escaping gear, wrapped in harmless-looking packages.) Rope, fezzes, and maps were the articles chiefly required, and these we purchased without much difficulty in restaurants where we were known. Robin and I were adepts at this sort of thing by now. One of us had only to go over to our escort's table, and standing over them, inquire whether they preferred black beer or yellow: meanwhile the other would be "wangling" the waiter. Besides material accessories we also required certain moral support. Was it worth while to escape? Would the Bulgarians attack Constantinople? What was the *morale* of the Tchatchaldja garrison? ... . All this and much more we learnt from Miss Whitaker, whom we met (just by chance, do you think?) at tea at the Petits Champs.

We returned from our excursion highly satisfied with our prospects. That evening we thanked the Commandant warmly for our delightful day, and asked one favour more, namely that we should be allowed out regularly into the garden, in order to get the exercise necessary to our health. An hour's walk every day would greatly relieve the tension of captivity. Surely, we said, the Commandant did not intend to keep us caged like wild beasts, with a minimum of air and exercise?

Permission was granted, with the proviso that we should not talk to other prisoners. Of all black sheep we were the blackest ones.

So we walked in the garden, and discussed plans of escape. We now had fezzes, rope, and plenty of money. On the other hand, there were so many sentries everywhere, and so many doors and barriers to get through, that the thing seemed impossible at first.

Bribery was not to be thought of. Any attempt in this direction would have sent us through the portals of the damned again, to await the end of the war in chains.

Only in the garden was there the slightest chance of success. Our chance, however, lay, as before, in the element of the unexpected.

On the far side of the garden from the prison were some iron railings, which overlooked a drop of from one hundred to two hundred feet, to a street below. These railings were spaced at just about the width of a man's head. We tested them at various points while apparently engaged in looking at the view, and made a note of the gaps most suitable to squeeze through. No one appeared to think it likely we would try to escape over a precipice. The six sentries in the garden therefore, whose sole duty it was to watch us, generally devoted their attention to seeing we did not talk to the Greek clerks who came into the restaurant to get their dinner of an evening. Beyond occasionally saying the magic word "*Yok*," they allowed us to do much what we liked at the other side of the garden, where our interests, they thought, could only be of an innocent nature.

At first our idea was to get through the railings and slide down a rope into the street, but there were practical difficulties about this. Thirty fathoms of rope are impossible to conceal on one's person. Besides, we thought of a better plan.

Having got through the railings, we would climb along outside them, past the garden, and along the wall of a printing-house, where their support still continued, until we reached the main square of the Seraskerat. Here we would squeeze back through the railings (for the drop was still too difficult to negotiate) and proceed as follows: We would stroll to the centre of the square, light cigars, and then suddenly altering our demeanour, hurry back to the staff garage where the military motor-cars were kept. The sentry on guard would certainly think we were chauffeurs.

With a guttural curse or two, we would start up a car, and drive directly to the Bulgarian frontier, or Dedeagatch, as the situation dictated. If anyone attempted to stop us on the way, we had only to say, "*Kreuzhimmel donnerwetter*," and open out the throttle. The plan was charming in its simplicity and *kolossal* in conception. We already imagined ourselves arriving with full details of the Constantinople defences, in a big Mercédès car. The plan was complete. We had only to do it!

Opportunity came one twilight evening, when we two were alone in the garden, with the six sentries, all rather sleepy, and the Damad, who had just returned from a hectic week-end up the Bosphorus. He was full of stories and news which we did not want to hear. For a time he bored us to tears talking of the war, but at last conversation flagged, and we bade him a cordial goodnight, making an appointment to see him again next day, which we trusted we would not be in a position to keep.

Then we edged to the far side of the garden, where the railings were. The six sleepy sentries were watching the stream of people going into the restaurant near the entrance gate. They paid no attention to us, and looked—rather sadly, I thought—at the Greeks who were coming in to have a square meal, a thing that they themselves could only dream of.

Feeling that the moment was too good to be lost, and yet somehow too good to be true, we stood by the railings, with our heads half through.

"Come on," said Robin cheerily.

I put my head through, and my flinching flesh followed a moment later. I hung over the drop and looked and listened tensely for any stir in the garden, expecting every moment to hear the clamour of sentries and the drone of bullets. But all was quiet. One sentry lit another's cigarette. A third was playing with a kitten. The others had their backs turned.

We clambered along, and reached the printing-house. We were out of sight of the sentries now, and the way seemed clear, across a patch of ivy, to a gap which would give us entrance to the main square. Once we had gained its comparative freedom, success, I felt, was certain.

But my hope was short-lived. The railings on the wall of the printing-house led past an open window, which we had not been able to see from the garden. At this window three Turks were sitting. They were officials of the printing-house no doubt, and were now engaged in discussing short drinks and the prospect of the Bosphorus. Had we interposed our bodies between them and the view, we would have been in a very unpleasant position. With one finger they could have pushed us down to the street a hundred feet below, or else detained us where we were, to wait like wingless flies until soldiers came to drag us back.

It was a horrid anti-climax, but we decided to go back. There was no alternative.

That return journey was quite hideous, for at any moment before we reached our gap a sentry might have seen us. And even if they had missed us at fifty yards (and we were a sitting shot against the sunset) we would have looked absolutely foolish and been abjectly helpless.

All went well, however. We squeezed back through the railings, and found ourselves in the prison garden again. Our attempt had failed. I felt as if someone had suddenly flattened me out with a rolling pin. But Robin was quite undismayed.

"Our luck is in," he said—"else we would have been spotted against those railings just now. Look, it is a full moon, like the last time we escaped. I bet we succeed to-night."

"I won't take your money," I said, hugely heartened, however.

Four of our sentries were smoking sadly, and looking into the restaurant, as boys look into a cake-shop. The fifth was standing by the gold-fish pond. The sixth leaned against the railings, about eighty yards away from us, looking out towards Galata Bridge.

After hurriedly dusting ourselves, we walked straight past him. He turned and glanced at his watch, and then at us.

"Just five minutes more," we urged—"we haven't had nearly enough exercise yet."

And we continued walking round the garden, breathlessly discussing plans.

The sentry nodded and sighed, then turned again to contemplate the Golden Horn.

Our one remaining chance was to walk straight out of the gate near the restaurant, into the main square. In moments of intense stress one can sometimes grasp the psychology of a situation in a flash. We saw into the minds of the sentries, I believe. They were bored and unsuspecting. A sort of prevision came to us that we would be mistaken for Greek employees of the Ministry, and could stroll unquestioned through the gate, if we acted instantly.

It was getting dark now. We slipped into a patch of shadow, threw away our hats, and taking out the fezzes which we always carried concealed under our waistcoats, we put them on our heads. Then we strolled on.

To understand our feelings, it must be remembered that no officer has ever before succeeded in escaping from this ancient prison. The Turks prided themselves on the fact. Recently, a political suspect had made a desperate dash for liberty by the same entrance as we now approached, but he had been caught before he reached the outer square. Good men had tried—but fools rush in where angels fear to tread. And we *knew*, by sheer faith, that we would not be stopped.

We walked very slowly now, stopping sometimes to gesticulate, after the manner of the Mediterranean peoples. What we said I have no idea, but I think I spoke *staccato* Italian, while Robin answered in Arabic imprecations. Near the gate I remember saying to him passionately in English: "For God's sake turn your trousers down," for to one's sensitive mind such an oddity of dress was certain to spell detection. This was idiotic, but my nerves were on edge.

Mingling with the Greeks who were coming out of the restaurant, we came at a very, very leisurely pace to the sentry-guarded gate. Everyone has a pass of course, both to enter and to leave this gate, but season ticket holders, so to speak, are rarely asked to produce their credentials.

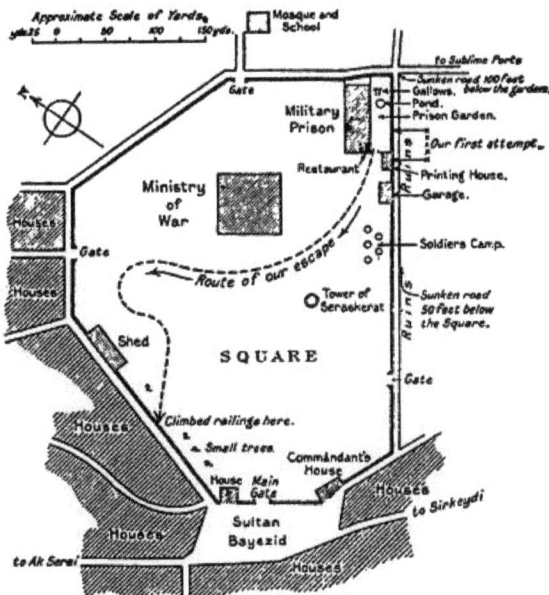

THE SQUARE OF THE SERASKERAT, CONSTANTINOPLE

We came level with the sentries at the gate. One of them took a step forward, as if to ask Robin a question. Then he looked at us again, and changed his mind. I have a sort of idea that my white waistcoat and ornamental watch chain saved the situation. No one with such belongings could fail to be a personage of clerkly habit.

In that instant, however, faith had almost faltered, and the temptation to quicken one's pace had been almost irresistible. To bolt into the comparative freedom of the main square was now quite feasible, but we had to remember that once there, our difficulties were only half over. Every gate was guarded: the same high railings as we had already negotiated formed its perimeter, and there was a battalion of soldiers in the square itself. Therefore until we were out of the Seraskerat, we had to proceed with caution.

Lethargically and nonchalantly we drew away from the restaurant. Although time was now a factor of importance (for at any moment the sentries in the garden might miss us), we dared not hurry our steps.

"There are no cars about. Are we going into the garage?" I murmured doubtfully to Robin.

At that moment an individual came up behind us, who settled the question out of hand. He was a Turkish officer. After passing us, he turned round to stare. We returned his scrutiny with careful composure, but it was quite obvious that he did not like the look of us. Yet our appearance was none of his business: he hesitated a moment and then decided to do exactly what one might do oneself if one saw a suspicious-looking individual in a public place: he went and told a policeman. We saw him hurrying to the main gate, where he called out the sergeant of the guard. We, meanwhile, were slinking diagonally across the square, as if bound for the side gate. To go to the garage now, as if approaching it from the Ministry of War, was impossible, as we were being watched. We whispered together, making new plans.

It was almost past twilight, but the electric light over the main gate showed us the Turkish officer in confabulation with the sergeant of the guard. No doubt he was saying that our passports should be scrutinised before we were allowed to pass. The sergeant saluted as the officer left, and then stood in the circle of light, a burly and menacing figure, peering into the gathering darkness.

We had now reached the middle of the Seraskerat and saw that the side gate was shut, and sentry-guarded. There was also a sentry in the adjacent shed. The main gate was impossible of access. So also was the garage. Our only chance lay in going forward.

We went on, past the shed, until we reached some small trees by the side of the outer railings. We tried to put our heads through, but owing to a slight difference of spacing, we found this could not be done. We would have to climb over them.

A couple of people were crossing the square. The sergeant stood blinking at the entrance. Else all was quiet.

The railings were only some twelve foot high, so they did not form a serious obstacle, but on their other side there was a drop of ten feet, into a crowded street. That someone would raise an alarm seemed very probable.

From the top of the railings I looked back to the prison where I had passed the last two months, and then forward to the street.

Two little girls stood hand in hand, gaping up at me. A street hawker glanced in my direction. Except for these, no passer-by appeared to notice us.

I dropped in a heap on the pavement. Next moment Robin landed beside me.

We were free once more, this time not to be recaught.

The two little girls clapped their hands with glee when they saw us drop. As to the street hawker, I daresay he thought we were robbers, and as such, people not to be interfered with. The other passers-by merely edged away from us. No one, in Constantinople, will involve himself in any civil commotion if he can avoid it. Whether the disturbance be a fire or theft, the procedure is the same. If your neighbour is being robbed, you look the other way. If your house is being burnt, you bribe the fire brigade not to come near it, for it they do, they will assuredly loot everything that the flames do not consume. Hence the sight of two wild men dropping into a crowded street stirred no civic conscience. No one asked who we were.

We crossed the tramway lines unmolested, and dived into a narrow street leading down the hill. Then we ran and ran and ran.

That our escape would be instantly reported we did not doubt. That Galata Bridge would be watched and all our old haunts also seemed certain. The care with which we had been guarded showed that the Turks set a value on keeping us out of harm's way. At large in the city we would be factors of unrest.

Avoiding main streets, we toiled on and on, through dark by-ways where the moonlight did not come, until we reached the old bridge across the Golden Horn. Here we decided to separate for the time, so that if one of us was caught by the toll-keepers, the other could still make good his escape.

But the toll-keepers took their tribute of a stamp without demur. They knew nothing of British prisoners.

Crossing, we turned right-handed, passing behind the American Ambassador's yacht *Scorpion*, at her berth near the Turkish Admiralty, and then went up into the European quarter. In Pera we knew a score of houses, between us, that would be glad to give us lodging, and it only remained to choose the most convenient.

It is late at night, some days before the Armistice. I am in the gardens of the British Embassy, with a certain Colonel, an escaped prisoner of war like myself, who is in close touch with the political situation. We had come here, in disguise, to be out of the turmoil of the town.

Outside, in the unquiet streets, men talk of revolution. Gangs of soldiers are under arms for twenty-four hours at a stretch. Machine guns are posted everywhere. The docks are an armed camp. Detectives and informers, the prison and the press-gang are at their old work. All is still dark in Constantinople; but we, fugitives at present, and meeting by stealth, speak of the day so soon to come when the barren flagstaff on the roof of the Embassy will carry the Union Jack.

Below us, as we walk on the terrace, lies the Golden Horn, silver in the starlight, and across its waters the city of Stamboul stands dim, forlorn, and lovely. The slip of moon that rides over San Sofia seems symbol of the waning of misery and intolerance. Soon that sickle will disappear, and when the moon of the Moslems rises again and looks through the garden where we talk, she will see all round it a happier city…. Let us hope so, anyway.

Of the maze of plot and counterplot in the city, of the death-throes of the old régime, and of our own small part in the history of that time, this record of moods and misadventures is not the place to write. My life as a prisoner was finished: my brief career as a minor diplomat, keeping his finger on the feverish pulse of Turkish politics, had only just begun, and the story of those crowded weeks would fill a volume.

Up to the last moment, the Government, in the person of Taalat Pasha, hoped to hold the real, if not the ostensible, reins of power. Until the flight of the Union and Progress triumvirate, the average Turk affected a certain lightheartedness about his country's losses. True, huge territories were lost to the Ottoman revenue, but on the other hand they had gained the Caucasus. So long as there was taxable territory, what did it matter whence the tribute came?

One night, when my newspaper work permitted, I visited a friend of Taalat Pasha, without disclosing my identity.

"Nobody but Taalat can possibly manage Turkey," he told me—"and the English, if they come, will be well advised to deal with him."

"It is not the English only," I suggested modestly, "but the whole world-set-free, that is coming to Constantinople."

"Then the world must deal with Taalat. His party has all the money, and all the brains and energy as well."

"Everything except imagination," I replied.

But I did not myself imagine that only thirty-six hours later Taalat, the fat telegraphist whom Fate caught in her toils, and Enver, with his peacock-grace and peacock-wits, and Djemal, with cruelty stamped on him like the brand of Cain, would pass disguised, and in darkness, and in fear of death, through the city they had ruled as kings.

Neither did I imagine that in another fortnight the streets of Pera would be decked with banners, and the capital of the Turks a playground for the peoples against whom they had lately been at war. Nor did I know that I should soon be listening to the strains of "Rule Britannia," at the Pera Palace Hotel, while an enthusiastic crowd showered confetti on the bald head of the Colonel who had just arrived as the first British representative. Nor did I know that I should telephone to the papers to stop their press, while I motored down with the first interview from our delegate. Nor, again, could I realise that the pomp of the Prussians would be so suddenly replaced by pipes and walking-sticks and dogs. Nor did I even dream that the fifty-sixty horse-power Mercédès car in which General Liman von Sanders was still racing through the streets would soon be my property, bought and paid for in gold, complete with all accessories, including even the chauffeur's diary, and that I should garage it in a garden where a performing bear stood guard against any attempt at theft by the disorderly and demoralised Germans. These things are another story.

Milton Keynes UK
Ingram Content Group UK Ltd.
UKHW011040240124
436589UK00003B/36